Hebrews

Developing Confidence for Reading the Letter

Let's Know the Bible Series
Herbert W. Bateman IV, general editor

God's Big Picture: An Overview of God's Developing Story (2014)
    Herbert W. Bateman IV, Timothy D. Sprankle, and Aaron C. Peer

The Gospels: Will the Real Jesus Please Stand Up (2015)
    Darrell L. Bock, Aaron C. Peer, and Jeremy Wike

Isaiah: Developing Confidence for Reading the Prophet Isaiah (2016)
    Robert B. Chisholm, Herbert W. Bateman IV, Aaron C. Peer, and Jeremy Wike

Hebrews: Developing Confidence for Reading the Letter (2018)
    George H. Guthrie and Herbert W. Bateman IV

Luke–Acts: Developing Confidence for Reading Luke's Writings (2018)
    Mark L. Strauss, Herbert W. Bateman IV, Timothy D. Sprankle, and Aaron C. Peer

Let's Know the Bible

Hebrews

Developing Confidence
for Reading the Letter

Herbert W. Bateman IV   George H. Guthrie

Herbert W. Bateman IV

General Editor

Hebrews: Developing Confidence in Reading and Studying the Letter to the Hebrews
© 2018 by Herbert W. Bateman IV

The Let's Know the Bible series is a reproduction of the September 8–9, 2017 Let's Know the Bible Conference Booklet created and edited by Herbert W. Bateman IV.

Published by Cyber-Center for Biblical Studies, 4078 E. Oldfield Drive, Leesburg, IN

"Scripture quotations are from the ESV® Bible (The Holy Bible, English Standard Version®), copyright © 2001 by Crossway, a publishing ministry of Good News Publishers. Used by permission. All rights reserved."

Scripture quoted by permission. Quotations designated (NET) are from the NET Bible® copyright ©1996-2016 by Biblical Studies Press, L.L.C. http://netbible.com All rights reserved.

Charts adapted from Herbert W. Bateman's *Charts on the Book of Hebrews* in Kregel Charts of the Bible (Grand Rapids: Kregel, 2012) used with permission.

All rights reserved. No part of this book may be reproduced or transmitted in any form or by any means—electronic, mechanical, photocopy, recording, or otherwise—without written permission of the author except for brief quotations in printed reviews.

ISBN 978-0-9907797-9-7

CONTENTS

Preface v

Conference Speaker viii

Conference Team Members ix

UNDERSTANDING THE NEW COVENANT
AS PRESENT IN JEREMIAH, UNDERSTOOD AT QUMRAN, AND FULFILLED IN HEBREWS

JEREMIAH AND THE NEW COVENANT *by Herbert W. Bateman IV*

- The Book of Jeremiah 3
  - General Chronology of the Prophets (Chart)
  - Jeremiah's References to Major Historical Figures (Chart)
- The Prophet Jeremiah 7
- Jeremiah & the New Covenant 11

QUMRAN AND THE NEW COVENANT *by Herbert W. Bateman IV*

- The Qumran Community 12
- Understandings of New Covenant 14
- Qumran and the New Covenant 15

HEBREWS AND THE NEW COVENANT *by George H. Guthrie*

- An Opening Illustration 18
- The Motivational Logic of Hebrews 18
- How New Covenant Fits in the Book of Hebrews 19
- Process: Longest Old Testament Quote in the New Testament 20

Why was There a Need 20
    The Concept of Covenant in Hebrews (Chart)
Three Key Elements of the New Covenant 22

THE BOOK OF HEBREWS

THREE WAYS TO TRANSFORM YOUR READING OF HEBREWS

George H. Guthrie

UNDERSTANDING THE BACKDROP OF HEBREWS

Introductions 25
Who Wrote this Book 25
    Potential Author of Hebrews First Identified (Chart)
To whom was the Book Written and When 29
    Debated Destinations of the Hebrews (Chart)
    Debated Considerations about the Dating (Chart)
How is Hebrews Relevant Today 32

TRACKING THE *CHRIST*-OLOGY

Introductions 33
How Hebrews Works 33
    Position and Character of Jesus as Regal Priest (Chart)
    Old Testament Quotations in Hebrews (Chart)
Four Main Movements of Hebrews *Christ*-ology 37

HEARING THE WORD OF ENCOURAGEMENT

Introductions 41
How Hebrews Works (with Exhortation) 41

    The Dangers of Apostasy in Hebrews (Chart)

    Views on the Warning Passages in Hebrews (Chart)

   Two Examples of Warning Passages 45

BUILDING CONFIDENCE IN READING THE BIBLE

READING A GOOD TRANSLATION

       by Aaron C. Peer 53

GRASPING GOD'S BIG PICTURE

       by Lee Compson 55

JESUS, GOD'S "DIFFERENT" PRIEST (HEBREWS 7:11)

       by Herbert W. Bateman IV 56

READ, RE-READ, AND READ AGAIN TO BUILD CONFIDENCE

       by Timothy D. Sprankle 57

READ THE BIBLE IN BIG CHUNKS

       by Michael Hontz 59

READ THE BIBLE WITH OTHERS

       by Lee Compson 60

READ THE BIBLE AS A FAMILY

       by Jeremy Wike 61

JESUS, OUR ETERNAL INTERCESSOR (HEBREWS 7:25)

       by Herbert W. Bateman IV 62

INCREASING A CONGREGATION'S BIBLE KNOWLEDGE

       by Timothy Sprankle 64

HOW PREACHING BUILDS CONFIDENCE IN THE BIBLE

       by Aaron Hoak 65

OUR MINISTER IN HEAVEN (HEBREWS 8:1–2)

       by Herbert W. Bateman IV 66

The Cyber-Center for Biblical Studies
Preface

We believe

the Bible is God's authoritative word for all followers of Jesus, the one through whom God has reestablished his Kingdom rule by means of Jesus' life, death, and resurrection, which is proclaimed clearly in the Bible.

Our Mission is

to promote the reading, studying, teaching, and preaching of the Bible.

We offer

- "A Pastor's Perspective" for reading and applying the Bible
- an annual conference for understanding the Bible one book at a time
- a free video library of resources for teachers and preachers of the Bible
- seminars for digging deeper the truths and applications of the Bible
- international theological training for preachers of the Bible
- books for guiding independent study of the Bible

Our offerings are

found on the Cyber-Center for Biblical Studies website: http://www.hwbateman.com

Our contact information is

Cyber-Center for Biblical Study
c/o Dr. Herbert W. Bateman IV
4078 E Old*ield Drive, Leesburg IN 46538
hwbatemaniv@gmail.com

We have

two administrators: Dr. Herbert W. Bateman IV (President) and Cindy Ann Bateman (Secretary-Treasurer), as well as a Let's Know the Bible Conference board of local pastors.

Preface

This book

Hebrews: Developing Con1idence for Reading the Letter is the reproduction of the September 8–9. 2017 Let's Know the Bible Conference booklet created and edited by Herbert W. Bateman IV in conjunction with George H. Guthrie and several Pastors serving in Northern Indiana.

To ensure that the conference targets a variety of local churches in the Northern Indiana area, the Let's Know the Bible has a volunteer board of pastors from churches ministering in Northern Indiana: **Lee Compson** of Milford First Brethren Church, Milford; **Michael Hontz** of Pleasant View Bible Church, Warsaw; **Aaron Peer** of Charter Oak Community Church, Churubusco; and **Timothy Sprankle** of Leesburg Grace Brethren Church, Leesburg.

Due to the mission of the Cyber-Center for Biblical studies, all Let's Know the Bible Conferences are videoed and available on the Cyber-Center's website: hwbateman.com. The Cyber-Center for Biblical Studies' video ministry has a national and international audience whereby pastors, teachers, missionaries, and students bene1it from the videoed Let's Know the Bible Conferences.

The videos that correspond with this book, *Hebrews: Developing for Reading the Letter*, may be found below.

- **Understanding the New Covenant: As Presented in Jeremiah, Understood at Qumran, and Ful-illed in Hebrews**

    by *Herbert W. Bateman IV and George H. Guthrie*

    YouTube: https://youtu.be/Mz5qhE2louk

    QR Code (it stands for "Quick Response") is a mobile phone readable barcode

Preface

- **Understanding the Backdrop of Hebrews**

    by *George H. Guthrie*

    YouTube: https://youtu.be/Xq39S-h9VMk

    QR Code (it stands for "Quick Response") is a mobile phone readable barcode

- **Tracking the Christ-ology in Hebrews**

    by *George H. Guthrie*

    YouTube: https://youtu.be/R16fHlatqrE

    QR Code (it stands for "Quick Response") is a mobile phone readable barcode

- **Hear the Word of Encouragement in Hebrews**

    by *George H. Guthrie*

    YouTube: https://youtu.be/_lRfJy1Cxx4

    QR Code (it stands for "Quick Response") is a mobile phone readable barcode

How to Activate the QR Code: Point a mobile phone (or other camera-enabled mobile) at the code. If the device has had QR Code decoding software installed on it, it will -ire up its browser and go straight to that URL.

vii

Preface

The Let's Know the Bible Team

HERBERT W. BATEMAN IV

Herb, founder of the Cyber-Center for Biblical Studies, has earned his B.S. in Biblical Studies from Cairn University (1982); his Th.M. (1987) and Ph.D. (1993) in New Testament Studies from Dallas Theological Seminary, and completed postdoctoral study at the University of Notre Dame.

He has been teaching Bible courses in academic institutions since 1986 and within the local church and on the mission field since 1978.

Herb has published fifteen books. Some of his publications include: *Authentic Worship* (Kregel, 2001), *Four Views on the Warning Passages in Hebrews* (Kregel, 2006), *Interpreting the Psalms for Preaching and Teaching* (Chalice, 2010), *Interpreting the General Letters* (Kregel, 2013), *Jude* in the Evangelical Exegetical Commentary series (Lexham, 2015), and *Understanding the Gospels: A Guide for Preaching and Teaching* (Kregel 2017).

Preface

CINDY ANN BATEMAN

Cindy, Vice President of Marketing at Lake City Bank, has earned her B.S. in Biblical Studies from Cairn University. She has studied at the University College Jerusalem Israel, and taken numerous courses for an MABS degree at Dallas Theological Seminary.

She has served as a short-term missionary in United Arab Emirates (1977), Philippines (1996), and Guatemala. Her community work involves Junior Achievement, CASA, and Big Brothers and Sisters. She has been an officer for the Cyber-Center for Biblical Studies and the treasurer for the Let's Know the Bible since 2014.

She is married with one child, Leah who is married to Travis Price and lives in Fort Worth, Texas.

R. W. LEE COMPSON

Lee, Senior Pastor at Milford First Brethren Church in Northern Indiana has earned his BS from Grace College (2003) and M.Div. degree from Grace Theological Seminary (2007).

He has been involved in vocational ministry since 2002 when he began as an intern at Pleasant View Bible Church focusing on college and young adult ministry. In January 2013, God led Lee and his wife Stephanie to Milford First Brethren where they enjoy serving and leading.

Lee was a contributing author to *Glimpses of Christ: Sermons from the Gospels* (Kainos Books, 2013), has written several articles for *The Voice* magazine, and has served as an instructor at Grace College. Lee joined the LKBC board in 2015.

Preface

MICHAEL HONTZ

Mike, Senior Pastor at Pleasant View Bible Church in Northern Indiana has earned his B.A. from Appalachian Bible College (2001) and his M.Div. from Grace Theological Seminary (2007).

He began as a Youth Pastor in Pennsylvania. After moving to Indiana, he began ministering at Pleasant View Bible Church as a pastoral intern in the areas of youth and music. After graduating from Grace Seminary, Mike became Pleasant View's Youth Pastor and eventually transitioned to become the Associate Pastor in 2009 and the Senior Pastor in 2011.

Mike has served as an instructor at Grace College and joined the LKBC board in 2016.

AARON C. PEER

Aaron, Senior Pastor at Charter Oak Church in Churubusco in Northern Indiana has earned his BA from Grace College (2000) and M.Div. degree from Grace Theological Seminary (2003).

He has taught Bible in academic and church settings since 1995 and pastored at Charter Oak for fourteen years. He has taught New Testament Greek and English Bible courses at Grace College and Theological Seminary, and spoken at conferences. Lee joined the LKBC board in 2014.

He assisted in the publication of *A Workbook for Intermediate Greek* by Herbert W. Bateman IV (Kregel, 2008) and co-authored *Translating 2 and 3 John Clause by Clause* (Cyber-Center for Biblical Studies, 2015), *God's Big Picture: An Overview of God's Developing Story* (Cyber-Center for Biblical Studies, 2015), and *Translating 1 John Clause by Clause* (Cyber-Center for Biblical Studies, 2017) with Herbert W. Bateman IV.

Preface

TIMOTHY D. SPRANKLE

Tim, Senior Pastor at Leesburg Grace Brethren Church in Northern Indiana has earned his BA from Grace College (2001) and M.Div. degree from Grace Theological Seminary (2004).

He has taught Bible in academic and church settings since 1995 and pastored for eleven years. Tim joined the LKBC board in 2014.

He has spoken at conferences, organized and directed plays, and read papers at Meetings of the Regional Midwest Evangelical Theological Society. He has an article published in *Authentic Worship* (Kregel 2001), and *Cyber-Center for Biblical Studies eJournal* (2014).

He is co-author of *God's Big Picture: An Overview of God's Developing Story* (Cyber-Center for Biblical Studies, 2015) and co-editor of the Cyber-Center for Biblical Studies' monthly posting of "A Pastor's Perspective" with Herbert W.   teman IV.

Hebrews Resources from Kregel Academic

"This collection of charts arranges, in easy format, information ranging from background, genre and structure, canonicity, influences from second temple Judaism, theological themes, and crucial exegetical issues. Laymen, students, pastors, and scholars will constantly refer to this work whenever they read, study, teach, or preach Hebrews. An indispensable resource."

—**David L. Allen**, Southwestern Baptist Theological Seminary

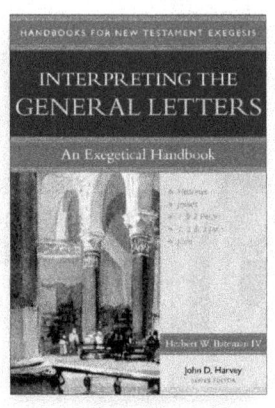

"Bateman presents a thorough process for exegesis of the Greek text of these letters, with examples and insights into the text that reinforce the value of doing the hard work of exegesis. This is a valuable introductory tool for students who are learning how to interpret the general letters and a trustworthy guide for pastors."

—**W. Edward Glenny**, University of Northwestern–St. Paul

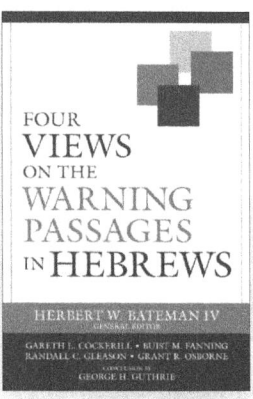

Join Grant Osborne, Buist Fanning, Gareth Cockerill, and Randall Gleason in this insightful examination of the five warning passages in Hebrews. Each of these esteemed New Testament scholars presents and defends his own viewpoint (Reformed, Wesleyan, or Arminian) and critiques the others. This unique volume helps clarify some of the most difficult passages of Scripture.

In these expositional and devotional lessons, the great heroes of the faith from Hebrews, chapter 11, glisten like twinkling stars in the night. Their shining examples of faith are vivid evidence of each believer's potential in Christ.

Conference Speakers

- GENERAL CONFERENCE SATURDAY MORNING: "The Book of Hebrews: Three Ways to Transform your Reading of Hebrews."

Dr. **George Howard Guthrie** (Ph.D. Southwestern Baptist Theological Seminary) is the Benjamin W. Perry Professor of Bible at Union University in Jackson, Tennessee. He was recently appointed as professor of New Testament at Regent College in Vancouver, British Columbia. An appointment he will begin in the Fall 2018.

Dr. Guthrie is considered to be one of the premier authorities in the United States on the Book of Hebrews. While an author of numerous articles and books, some of his most notable works in Hebrews are: *Hebrews: Running the Race Before Us (Bringing the Bible to Life)*, co-authored-edited with Janet Nygren (Zondervan, 2008); *Hebrews,* Commentary on the New Testament Use of the Old Testament, edited by D. A. Carson and G. K. Beale (Baker Academic, 2007); *Hebrews* in Hebrews-Revelation volume of the Zondervan Illustrated Backgrounds Commentary (Zondervan, 2002); *Hebrews,* NIV Application Commentary Series (Zondervan. 1998); *The Structure of Hebrews: A Text-linguistic Analysis*, Supplements to Novum Testamentum, 73 (E. J. Brill, 1994).

Dr. Guthrie's website George H. Guthrie: Helping you Read the Bible Better (georgehguthrie.com) provides numerous suggestions for building confidence in reading the Bible.

- PRE–CONFERENCE FRIDAY EVENING: "Understanding the New Covenant: As Presented in Jeremiah, Understood at Qumran, and Fulfilled in Hebrews"

Dr. Guthrie is joined by Dr. Herbert W. Bateman IV for the Pre–Conference Event Friday evening.

Dr. **Herbert W. Bateman IV** (Ph.D. Dallas Theological Seminary) is President of the Cyber-Center for Biblical Studies. He has been teaching Bible courses in academic institutions since 1986 and within the local church and on the mission field since 1978.

He has spoken at various conferences and written for the church and the academy. Some of his works on the Book of Hebrews are *Interpreting the General Letters* (Kregel, 2013), *Charts on the Book of Hebrews,* Kregel Charts of the Bible (2012), *Four Views on the Warning Passages in Hebrews*, ed. (Kregel, 2006), *Early Jewish Hermeneutics and Hebrews 1:5–13*, Theology and Religion, 193 (Peter Lang, 1997).

HERBERT W. BATEMAN IV

UNDERSTANDING THE NEW COVENANT:

AS PRESENTED IN JEREMIAH, UNDERSTOOD AT QUMRAN, AND FULFILLED IN HEBREWS

HERBERT W. BATEMAN IV
GEORGE H. GUTHRIE

JEREMIAH & THE NEW COVENANT

1. THE BOOK OF JEREMIAH

A. AN OUTLINE FOR THE BOOK OF JEREMIAH

1) Introduction—Jeremiah's _____ (chp. 1)

2) Prophecies to the Nation of _____ (chps. 2–44)

   "I will punish"
   "I will restore"

2) Prophecies to the _____ (chps. 45–51)

4) The Fall of _____ (chp. 52)

The Book of Jeremiah							
1	2						44	45 51	52
Jeremiah's Call	Prophecies to the Leaders of Judah and Jerusalem						Prophecies about the Gentiles	Jerusalem's Fall
Prophetic Commission	Messages of Judgment	Messages of Captivity	Messages of Restoration	Jerusalem's Captivity & Fall	Messages to the Remnant	Messages against the Gentiles	Historical Conclusion
1	2 20	26 29	30 33	34 39	40 44	45 51	52
Before the Fall of Jerusalem						After the Fall of Jerusalem	

Cyber-Center for Biblical Studies © 2017

B. CONTEMPORARY READERS OF JEREMIAH BEWARE

1) Jeremiah is _____ arranged in chronological order.

KING	CHAPTERS				
Josiah	1–20				
Jehoiakim		25–26	35–36	45	46–51
Zedekiah	21–24	27–34	37–39		or 46–51
Gedaliah				40–42	
Egypt				43–44	

2) The fourth year of Jehoiakim is mentioned _____ times (25:1; 36:1; 45:1; 46:2)

The fourth year of Jehoiakim is very important because it is the year King Nebucahnezzar came to power.

3) Jeremiah's Original _____.

All of Jeremiah's messages were preached to the leaders of Judah and Jerusalem prior to King Nebuchadnezzar's

final _____ of the people,

the ultimate _____ of the city,

and the _____ of David's dynasty.

4) Original _____ of the Book of Jeremiah

The original readers of Jeremiah were the Jewish people who had been carried off into exile and served as a reminder that **restoration** is coming (cf. Daniel 9:1–2).

GENERAL CHRONOLOGY OF THE PROPHETS

PROPHET	ESTIMATED MINISTRY	PERIOD	AUDIENCE	
Amos	767 – 753	Pre-Exile	Northern Israel	A S S Y R I A 900 TO 612
Hosea	755 – 715	Pre-Exile	Northern Israel	
Micah	735 – 701	Israel's in Exile Pre-Exile Judah	Judah	
Isaiah	739 – 685	Pre-Exile	Judah	
Nahum	663 – 612	Israel's in Exile Pre-Exile Judah	Nineveh / Assyria	
Zephaniah	632 – 628	Israel's in Exile Pre-Exile Judah	Judah	
Habakkuk	626 – 609	Israel's in Exile Pre-Exile Judah	Judah	
Jeremiah	**605 – 586**	**Israel's in Exile Pre-Exile Judah**	**Judah**	B A B Y L O N 612 TO 539
Daniel	605 – 535	Judah in Exile	Judah	
Ezekiel	597 – 571	Judah in Exile	Judah	
Obadiah	After 586	Judah in Exile	Edom	
Jonah	??	Judah in Exile	(about) Nineveh	
Haggai	520 – 520	Post-Exile	Returned Jews	P E R S I A
Zechariah	520 – 480	Post-Exile	Returned Jews	
Joel	515	Post-Exile	Judah	
Malachi	450	Post-Exile	Returned Jews	

Dating Source: Robert B. Chisholm, *Interpreting the Minor Prophets* (Zondervan, 1990)
Chart Created by Herbert W. Bateman IV (Leesburg, IN: Cyber-Center for Biblical Studies, 2016)

JEREMIAH'S REFERENCES TO MAJOR HISTORICAL EVENTS

YEAR	FINAL YEARS OF JUDAH
627	God calls Jeremiah to be a prophet during the reign of King Josiah (Jer. 1:2-3)
605	**First Deportation**: Nebuchadnezzar takes Daniel, Hananiah, Mishael, and Azariah and other royal family members and nobles to Babylon as his captives (Dan 1:1-2; Jer 25:1, 3, 8-12; 46:2).
598	Nebuchadnezzar invades Judah and lays siege on Jerusalem (Dec.). Judah's King Jehoiakim dies during the siege (Dec. 9).
597	**Second Deportation**: Jehoiakim's son, Jehoiachin, ascends to the throne, reigns three months ten days, before deported to Babylon along with Ezekiel (2 Kgs. 24:8-14; 2 Chron. 36:9-10; Josephus, *Antiquities* 10.6.3 § 98). Nebuchadnezzar appoints Zedekiah, as king over Judah.
596	**Jeremiah's Warning**: Jeremiah warns Zedekiah not to join forces with Edom, Moab, Ammon, Tyre and Sidon, against Nebuchadnezzar (Jer. 27:1-11).
	Jeremiah and Ezekiel tell the people to settle in Babylon (Jer. 28-29; Ezek. 13), even though false prophets were predicting Nebuchadnezzar's defeat.
586	**Third Deportation**: Nebuchadnezzar invades Judah and lays siege on Jerusalem (Jan. 15, 586 B.C.; 2 Kgs. 25:1-2; Jer. 52:4-5; Ezek. 24:1-14).
	On 18 July, a famine brakes out in Jerusalem (2 Kgs. 25:3; Jer. 39:2). Shortly thereafter, Jerusalem's walls were breached, Zedekiah's were family was killed before him, he was blinded, chained and carried off to Babylon (2 Kgs. 25:3-7; Jer. 52:6-11).

The Last Kings of Judah during Jeremiah's Ministry

Josiah (640-609 B.C.)

Jehoahaz (Shallum; 609 B.C.)

Jehoiakim (609-596 B.C.)

Jehoiachin (597 B.C.)

Zedekiah (597-586 B.C.)

Nebuchadnezzar
King of Babylon

In 605 B.C., Prince Nebuchadnezzar defeated the Assyrian and the Egyptian armies at Carchemish in 605 B.C.

During Prince Nebuchadnezzar's pursuit of the Egyptians through Syria and Judea, his father died August 15, 605 B.C.

Prince Nebuchadnezzar halted his campaign, returned to Babylon, and ascended to the throne of Babylon September 7, 605 B.C.

God's Servant

⁴... `This is what the LORD Almighty, the God of Israel, says: "Tell this to your masters: ⁵With my great power and outstretched arm I made the earth and its people and the animals that are on it, and I give it to anyone I please. ⁶Now *I will hand all your countries over to **my servant Nebuchadnezzar** king of Babylon; I will make even the wild animals subject to him.* ⁷All nations will serve him and his son and his grandson until the time for his land comes; then many nations and great kings will subjugate him. ⁸"If, however, any nation or kingdom will not serve Nebuchadnezzar king of Babylon or bow its neck under his yoke, I will punish that nation with the sword, famine and plague, declares the LORD, until I destroy it by his hand. Jeremiah 27:4-8 (NIV)

Let's Know the Bible Conference: Hebrews

2. THE PROPHET JEREMIAH

A. JEREMIAH'S BEGINNINGS

1) Jeremiah was a _____, from a priestly family, from the city of Anathoth in geographical territory of Benjamin (1:1).

2) Jeremiah was called by God to be a _____ in 627 B.C. during the reign of King Josiah (1:2–3).

```
Priest

Prophet
```

B. JEREMIAH'S CALLING

1) Jeremiah's _____ (1:4–5).

> ⁴Now the word of the Lord came to me, saying, ⁵"Before I formed you in the womb I knew you, and before you were born I consecrated you; I appointed you a prophet to the nations." (ESV)

2) Jeremiah's _____ (1:6).

> ⁶Then I said, "Ah, Lord God! Behold, I do not know how to speak, for I am only a youth." (ESV)

Michelangelo's depiction of Jeremiah, Sistine Chapel ceiling

3) God's _____ (1:7–10).

> ⁷But the Lord said to me, "Do not say, 'I am only a youth'; for to all to whom I send you, you shall go, and whatever I command you, you shall speak.

⁸Do not be afraid of them, for I am with you to deliver you, declares the Lord."

⁹Then the Lord put out his hand and touched my mouth. And the Lord said to me, "Behold, I have put my words in your mouth. ¹⁰See, I have set you this day over nations and over kingdoms, **to pluck up and to break down, to destroy and to overthrow**, **to build and to plant**." (ESV)

C. JEREMIAH'S TWOFOLD MESSAGE

1) Jeremiah's message of _____.

The Mosaic Covenant was to be _____ (11:1-8)

¹The word that came to Jeremiah from the Lord:

²"Hear the words of this covenant, and speak to the men of Judah and the inhabitants of Jerusalem. ³You shall say to them, Thus says the Lord, the God of Israel: Cursed be the man who does not hear the words of this covenant ⁴that I commanded your fathers when I brought them out of the land of Egypt, from the iron furnace, saying, Listen to my voice, and do all that I command you. So shall you be my people, and I will be your God, ⁵that I may confirm the oath that I swore to your fathers, to give them a land flowing with milk and honey, as at this day." Then I answered, "So be it, Lord."

⁶And the Lord said to me, "Proclaim all these words in the cities of Judah and in the streets of Jerusalem: Hear the words of this covenant and do them. ⁷For I solemnly warned your fathers when I brought them up out of the land of Egypt, warning them persistently, even to this day, saying, Obey my voice. ⁸Yet they did not obey or incline their ear, but everyone walked in the stubbornness of his evil heart. Therefore I brought upon them all the words of this covenant, which I commanded them to do, but they did not."

Conspiracy against the Mosaic Covenant will lead to ruin (11:9-17)

⁹Again the Lord said to me, "A conspiracy exists among the men of Judah and the inhabitants of Jerusalem. ¹⁰They have turned back to the iniquities of their forefathers, who refused to hear my words. They have gone after other gods to serve them. The house of Israel and the house of Judah have broken my covenant that I made with their fathers. ¹¹Therefore, thus says the Lord, Behold, I am bringing disaster upon them that they cannot escape. Though they cry to me, I will not listen to them. ¹²Then the cities of Judah

and the inhabitants of Jerusalem will go and cry to the gods to whom they make offerings, but they cannot save them in the time of their trouble. ¹³For your gods have become as many as your cities, O Judah, and as many as the streets of Jerusalem are the altars you have set up to shame, altars to make offerings to Baal.

¹⁴"Therefore do not pray for this people, or lift up a cry or prayer on their behalf, for I will not listen when they call to me in the time of their trouble. "Hear the words of this covenant, and speak to the men of Judah and the inhabitants of Jerusalem. (ESV)

The consequence for _____ the Mosaic Law (17:1-4)

¹"The sin of Judah is written with a pen of iron; with a point of diamond it is engraved on the tablet of their heart, and on the horns of their altars, ²while their children remember their altars and their Asherim, beside every green tree and on the high hills, ³on the mountains in the open country. Your wealth and all your treasures I will give for spoil as the price of your high places for sin throughout all your territory. ⁴You shall loosen your hand from your heritage that I gave to you, and I will make you serve your enemies in a land that you do not know, for in my anger a fire is kindled that shall burn forever." (ESV)

Jeremiah Lamenting the Destruction of Jerusalem by Rembrandt (1630)

2) Jeremiah's message of _____.

The Lord will restore his people to the _____ (29:10–14)

¹⁰"For thus says the Lord: When seventy years are completed for Babylon, I will visit you, and I will fulfill to you my promise and bring you back to this place. ¹¹For I know the plans I have for you, declares the Lord, plans for welfare and not for evil, to give you a future and a hope. ¹²Then you will call upon me and come and pray to me, and I will hear you. ¹³You will seek me and find me, when you seek me with all your heart. ¹⁴I will be found by you, declares the Lord, and I will restore your fortunes and gather you from all the nations and all the places where I have driven you, declares the Lord, and I will bring you back to the place from which I sent you into exile. (ESV)

The Lord will restore the city of _____ (30:18–22)

¹⁸"Thus says the Lord: Behold, I will restore the fortunes of the tents of Jacob and have compassion on his dwellings; the city shall be rebuilt on its mound, and the palace shall stand where it used to be. ¹⁹Out of them shall come songs of thanksgiving, and the voices of those who celebrate. I will multiply them, and they shall not be few; I will make them honored, and they shall not be small.

²⁰Their children shall be as they were of old, and their congregation shall be established before me, and I will punish all who oppress them. ²¹Their prince shall be one of themselves; their ruler shall come out from their midst; I will make him draw near, and he shall approach me, for who would dare of himself to approach me? declares the Lord. ²²And you shall be my people, and I will be your God." (ESV)

The Lord will restore David's _____ (33:14–18)

¹⁴"Behold, the days are coming, declares the Lord, when I will fulfill the promise I made to the house of Israel and the house of Judah. ¹⁵In those days and at that time I will cause a righteous Branch to spring up for David, and he shall execute justice and righteousness in the land. ¹⁶In those days Judah will be saved, and Jerusalem will dwell securely. And this is the name by which it will be called: 'The Lord is our righteousness.'

¹⁷"For thus says the Lord: David shall never lack a man to sit on the throne of the house of Israel, ¹⁸and the Levitical priests shall never lack a man in my presence to offer burnt offerings, to burn grain offerings, and to make sacrifices forever." (ESV)

The Lord will make a _____ with Israel (31:31–34)

³¹"Behold, the days are coming, declares the Lord, when I will make a new covenant with the house of Israel and the house of Judah, ³²*not like* the covenant that I made with their fathers on the day when I took them by the hand to bring them out of the land of Egypt, my covenant that they broke, ʳthough I was their husband, declares the Lord. ³³For this is the covenant that I will make with the house of Israel after those days, declares the Lord: I will put my law within them, and I will write it ᵗon their hearts. ᵘAnd I will be their God, and they shall be my people. ³⁴And no longer shall each one teach his neighbor and each his brother, saying, 'Know the Lord,' for they shall all know me, from the least of them to the greatest, declares the Lord. For I will forgive their iniquity, and I will remember their sin no more." (ESV)

Let's Know the Bible Conference: Hebrews

3. JEREMIAH AND THE NEW COVENANT

A. THE NEW COVENANT IS **ONE-_____**. OF MANY DIVINE PROMISES OF RESTORATION

　1) The Lord will restore his people to the _____.

　2) The Lord will restore the city of _____.

　3) The Lord will restore David's _____.

　4) The Lord will make a _____ _____ with Israel.

Prophet Jeremiah by Jeremiah Theus (1716-1774)

B. THE NEW COVENANT IS A **ONE-_____** COVENANT THAT GOD PROMISES TO MAKE WITH HIS PEOPLE

　1) I will _____ a new covenant with the house of Israel and the house of Judah, *not like* the covenant that I made with their fathers

　2) I will _____ my law within them

　3) I will _____ it on their hearts

　4) I will be their _____, and they shall be my people

　5) I will _____ their iniquity

　6) I will _____ their sin no more

QUMRAN & THE NEW COVENANT

1. THE QUMRAN COMMUNITY

A. _____ OVERVIEW

The **Dead Sea region** has yielded many exciting and valuable discoveries for twentieth century archaeologists. For instance, Wadi Qumran, Murabba'at and Nahal Hever yielded many artifacts and documents con- cerning Bar-Kokhba's revolt (135 CE).

Qumran sits on a plateau that overlooks the Dead Sea, While the Qumran is about 1,300 feet below sea level, the Dead Sea is another 1,000 feet below the Qumran. The nearby cliffs and caves cut by Wadi Qumran provided a well-protected hiding place for the now famous Dead Sea Scrolls.

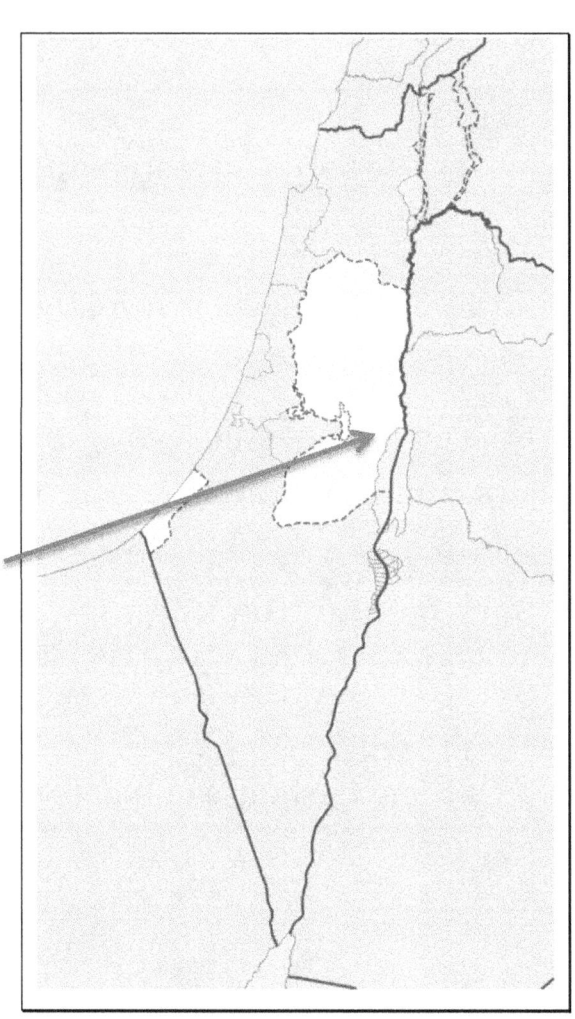

Qurman

Map of Present-day Israel

B. _____ OVERVIEW

It is believed a Jewish religious sect known as the Essenes settled Qumran as early as 134 B.C. The Romans later destroyed the settlement in A.D. 68 as a result of the Jewish war.

Let's Know the Bible Conference: Hebrews

C. _____ OVERVIEW

The earliest manuscripts and numerous fragments were found in a cave by Bedouin in April 1947.

Two years latter, 1949, European Archaeologists began investigating the area for other scrolls and fragments.

Discoveries at Qumran		Fragments
1*	**Bedouin**, 1947	82 (17 biblical)
2	Bedouin, 1952	33 (18 biblical)
3	Archaeologists, 1952	15 (3 biblical)
4*	**Bedouin**, 1952	434+ (169 biblical)
5	Archaeologists, 1952	25 (8 biblical)
6	Bedouin, 1952	31 (7 biblical)
7	Archaeologists, 1955	19 (2 biblical)
8	Archaeologists, 1955	5 (2 biblical)
9	Archaeologists, 1955	1
10	Archaeologists, 1955	1
11*	**Bedouin**, 1956	25 (10 biblical)

Not all the Dead Sea Scroll manuscripts and fragments found in the caves surrounding the Qumran settlement are considered literature originally composed at Qumran. The Dead Sea Scroll material is divided into one of two categories. They are classified as either:

1) sectarian writing of the _____ (community rule, war scroll, etc.),

2) popular _____ writings (*Jubilees*, Enoch, Tobit, etc.),

3) Old Testament _____ writings (all except Esther and Nehemiah).

Cyber-Center for Biblical Studies © 2017

2. UNDERSTANDINGS OF THE NEW COVENANT[1]

A. THE NEW COVENANT WAS A _____ COVENANT BETWEEN GOD AND HIS PEOPLE

1) The New Covenant was viewed, by some Jews of Jesus day, as a renewal and an updated version of previous covenants that God had entered into with Jewish ancestors. For instance, the first law was given to Noah and his sons (*Jubilees* 6), that law was supplemented with God's commands about circumcision (*Jubilees* 15), those laws were increased to include procedures for executing sacrifices (*Jubilees* 21), to those laws was added the separation of Jewish people from Gentiles (*Jubilees* 30).

2) God's laws, inherited from generation to generation, were considered to be a mutual covenantal agreement between God and their Jewish ancestors rather than a promissory covenant from God.

> **The Book of *Jubilees***
>
> The book of *Jubilees* is a non-biblical Jewish book. It was compose around 160–150 B.C. before Qumran was settled by a group of Essenes. It contains the retelling of the biblical books of Genesis and Exodus 1–19.
>
> *Jubilees* opens with God conversing with Moses about Israel's future disobedience and God's restoration of the nation (chp. 1). Yet it shifts to an angel who then reveals the contents of some heavenly tablets to Moses (chps. 2–50).
>
> The author of *Jubilees* places the biblical stories into story units that are of forty-nine year duration, called jubilees. Several copies of the book were found at Qumran. It is not, however, a book composed by or at Qumran.

B. THE NEW COVENANT WAS _____.

1) Inauguration of the New Covenant was achieved by way of _____.

2) Inauguration of the New Covenant was achieved by and the taking of an _____ to perform and obey God's commandments.

---

[1] This section "The New Covenant Misunderstandings" and Qumran and the New Covenant" is derived from (1) Bilhah Nitzan's "The Concept of the Covenant in Qurman Literature in the Historical Perspective of the Covenant between God and Israel (Tel-Aviv University); (2) James C. VanderKam, "Covenant" in *Encyclopedia of the Dead Sea Scrolls Volume 1*, edited by Lawrence H. Schiffman and James C. VanderKam (New York, NY: Oxford University Press, 2000), 151–55.

Let's Know the Bible Conference: Hebrews

C. THE NEW COVENANT WAS _____

The mutual covenantal agreement between God and Israel – that the Jewish people become God's special possession from all people and that they be a kingdom of priests and holy people — was already predestined.

3. QUMRAN & THE NEW COVENANT

A. THE QUMRANIANS WERE THE "NEW _____"

The Jewish people who settled at Qumran viewed themselves as God's covenantal people of the new covenant. This belief is evident in a document composed by them and before they moved to Qumran. It was while they were living in Damascus, that someone of their community wrote a document that describes them as God's new covenant people.

1) People who have been _____ into the covenant

... must be careful to act according to the specifications of the Law ..., avoiding filthy wicked lucre taken from what is vowed or consecrated to God or found in the Temple funds.

They must not rob "the poor of God's people, making widows' wealth their booty and killing orphans" (Isaiah 10:2).

They must distinguish between defiled and pure, teaching the difference between holy and profane.

They must keep the Sabbath day according to specification and the holy days and the fast day according to the commandments of

The Damascus Document (CD)

The Damascus Document (CD) is a Qumran sectarian text divided into two major sections: "The Admonition," and "The Law and Communal Rules."

"The Admonition" reviews Israelite history by focusing on Israel's past and future punishment as well as God's gracious salvation of Israel's "remnant" (1:1-10; also referred to as "a sure house in Israel" in 3:19, "the House of Judah" in 4:11, and "those who entered the new covenant in the land of Damascus" in 6:19, cf. 6:5, 7:19).[1]

The appeal to the three historical tragedies in "the Admonition," where the text speaks of God's future punishment of wicked backsliders, is intentionally used to warn readers to stay firm in the Jewish tradition and not to stray from it, namely, "The Law and Communal Rules."

the *members of the new covenant* in the land of Damascus, offering the holy things according to their specifications. (CD 6:11–18)[2]

2) So there is one _____ for everyone who rejects the commandments of God and abandons them to follow their own willful heart. This is the word that Jeremiah spoke to Baruch son of Neriah, and Elisha to Gehazi his servant. (So it is with) all the men *who entered the new covenant* in the land of Damascus. (CD 8:18–21)[3]

3) God loved the _____ who bore witness to the people following God, so too He loves those who follow them, for to such belongs the covenant of the fathers. So there is one fate for everyone who rejects the commandments of God [...] and abandons them to follow their own willful heart. So it is with *all the men who entered the new covenant* in the land of Damascus, but then turned back and traitorously turned away from the fountain of living water. (CD 19:29–30; 32–34)[4]

B. QUMRAN'S UNDERSTANDINGS OF THE NEW COVENANT

---

[2] The translation is from Michael Wise, Martin Abegg Jr., Edward Cook, *The Dead Sea Scrolls: A New Translation* (New York: HarperCollins, 1996): 56–57. For another translation see, Florentino García Martínez and Eibert J.C. Tigchelaar, *The Dead Sea Scrolls: Study Edition Volume 1 (1Qq–4Q273)* (Grand Rapids: Eerdmans, 1997), 559.

[3] Wise, Abegg, Cook, 59; for Martinez and Eibert, 563.

[4] Ibid..

Let's Know the Bible Conference: Hebrews

SO WHAT?

Jeremiah's prophecy was _____.

Jesus taught something _____.

Luke 22:14–20

[14] Now when the hour came, Jesus took his place at the table and the apostles joined him. [15] And he said to them, "I have earnestly desired to eat this Passover with you before I suffer. [16] For I tell you, I will not eat it again until it is fulfilled in the kingdom of God." (NET)

[17] Then he took a cup, and after giving thanks he said, "Take this and divide it among yourselves. [18] For I tell you that from now on I will not drink of the fruit of the vine until the kingdom of God comes." [19] Then he took bread, and after giving thanks he broke it and gave it to them, saying, "This is my body which is given for you. Do this in remembrance of me." [20] And in the same way he too the cup after they had eaten, saying, *This cup that is poured out for you is the **new covenant** in my blood.* (NET)

1 Corinthians 11:23–26

[23] For I received from the Lord what I also passed on to you, that the Lord Jesus on the night in which he was betrayed took bread, [24] and after he had given thanks he broke it and said, "This is my body, which is for you. Do this in remembrance of me." [25] In the same way, he also took the cup after supper, saying, *"This cup is the **new covenant** in my blood.* Do this, every time you drink it, in remembrance of me." [26] For every time you eat this bread and drink the cup, you proclaim the Lord's death until he comes. (NET)

HEBREWS & THE NEW COVENANT

1. AN OPENING ILLUSTRATION:

2. THE MOTIVATIONAL LOGIC OF HEBREWS

   A. Your Perseverance in the Christian life will be in direct proportion to the _____ with which you see _____ Jesus is and _____ he has accomplished on our behalf.

   B. Jesus has brought about a _____ and superior way of _____ to God.

   C. So, _____ in following Jesus!

3. HOW NEW COVENANT FITS IN THE BOOK OF HEBREWS

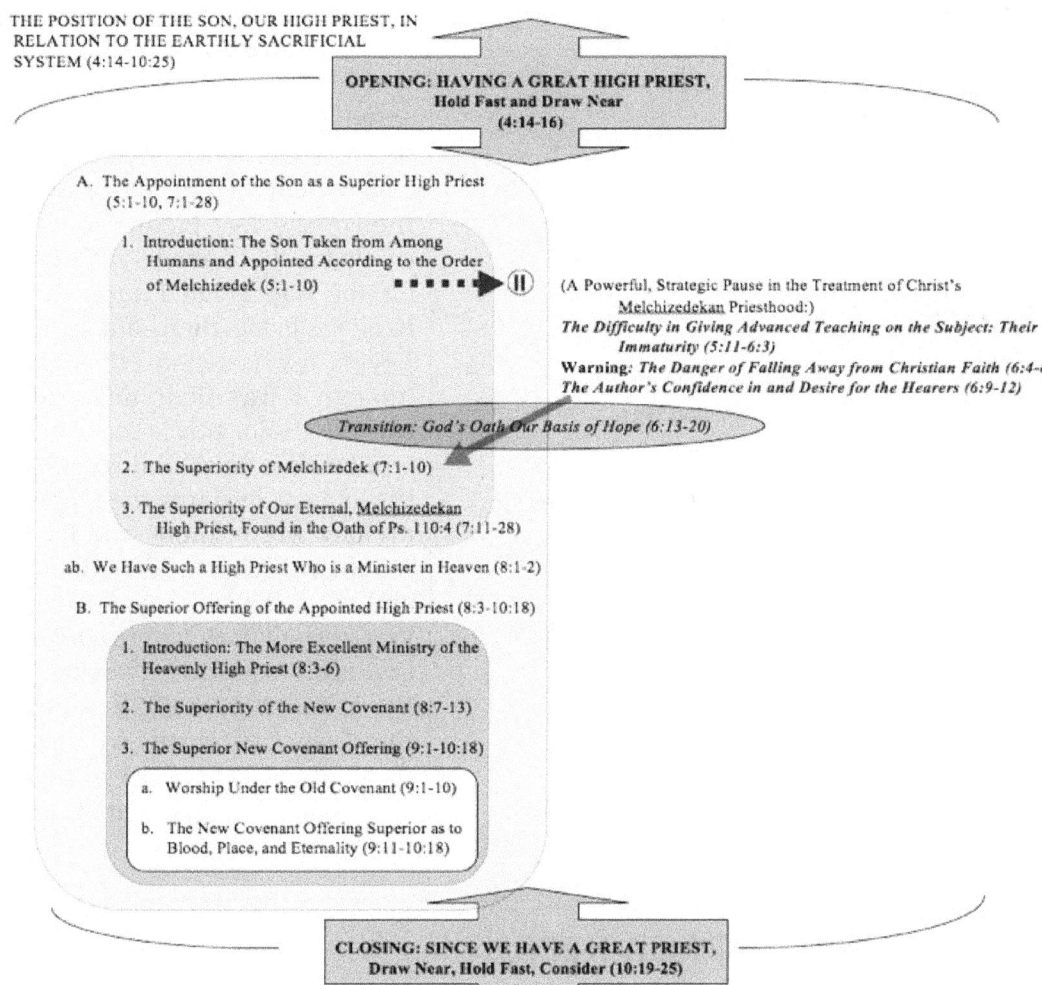

Let's Know the Bible Conference: Hebrews

4. **PROCESS**: LONGEST _____ IN THE NEW TESTAMENT (JER. 31:31-34)

A rabbinic technique:

Capitalizes on the word

_____

> **Jeremiah 31:31–34**
>
> ³¹"Behold, the days are coming, declares the Lord, when I will make a new covenant with the house of Israel and the house of Judah, ³²not like the covenant that I made with their fathers on the day when I took them by the hand to bring them out of the land of Egypt, my covenant that they broke, ʳthough I was their husband, declares the Lord. ³³For this is the covenant that I will make with the house of Israel after those days, declares the Lord: ˢI will put my law within them, and I will write it ᵗon their hearts. ᵘAnd I will be their God, and they shall be my people. ³⁴And no longer shall each one teach his neighbor and each his brother, saying, 'Know the Lord,' for they shall all know me, from the least of them to the greatest, declares the Lord. For I will forgive their iniquity, and I will remember their sin no more." (ESV)

5. WHY WAS THERE A NEED?

THE CONCEPT OF COVENANT IN HEBREWS[1]

"Covenant" (διαθήκη) in Hebrews		
The Covenant is . . .	better	7:22; 8:6
	founded of better promises	8:16
	New	
	καινήν	8:8 (via Jeremiah 31:31)
		8:13 (implied)
		9:15
	νέας	12:24
	not like the covenant made with their forefathers	8:9 (via Jeremiah 31:32)
	prophesied for 'that time'	8:10; 10:16 (via Jeremiah 31:33)
	like a 'will' in force at the death of the one who made it	9:16, 17
	put into effect with the blood of Jesus	9:20; 10:29; 13:20
	eternal	13;20
Jesus is . .	the guarantee	7:22
	the mediator	8:6; 9:15; 12:24
	the one who made it [and whose death put into effect]	9:17
For those who are called . . .	receive the promised eternal inheritance	9:15
	are set free from sin	10:29
For those who the blood of Jesus as unholy . . .	deserve severe punishment	9:15

[1] Adapted from Herbert W. Bateman IV, *Charts on the Book of Hebrews* in Kregel Charts of the Bible (Grand Rapid: Kregel, 2012), 125.

6. 3 KEY ELEMENTS OF THE NEW COVENANT:

A. The Law of God _____

B. Personal Relationship _____

C. Decisive Forgiveness _____

How was the Offering of Jesus Superior?

1.

2.

3.

7.   APPLICATION

THE BOOK OF HEBREWS:

THREE WAYS TO TRANSFORM YOUR READING OF HEBREWS

GEORGE H. GUTHRIE

UNDERSTAND THE BACKDROP OF HEBREWS

1. **INTRODUCTION**

   The Story of Antonius

   The Foundational Message of Hebrews

   "Your perseverance in the Christian faith will be in direct proportion to the ***clarity*** with which you see ***who Jesus is*** and ***what he has accomplished*** on our behalf!"
   George H. Guthrie

2. **WHO WROTE THIS BOOK?**

   A. Views on Authorship

B. Why Not Paul?

C. What Do We Know?

D. A Best Guess?

> "Now a Jew named Apollos, **a native of Alexandria**, arrived in Ephesus. He was an **eloquent speaker** [ἀνὴρ λόγιος], **well-versed in the scriptures**. He had been instructed in the way of the Lord, and with great enthusiasm he spoke and taught accurately the facts about Jesus, although he knew only the baptism of John. **He began to speak out fearlessly in the synagogue**, . . . [when he moved to Achaia] . . . he **refuted the Jews vigorously in public debate**, demonstrating from the scriptures that the Christ was Jesus." (Acts 18:28 NET)

POTENTIAL AUTHOR OF HEBREWS FIRST IDENTIFIED[1]

Suggested Author	Proponent	Date	Source
Barnabas	Tertullian	ca 150–220	*De pudicitia*, 20; *On Purity* in ACW 28.115, 277.
Paul	Pantaenus	ca 190	Eusebius, *Ecclesiastical History*, 6.14.4
Paul (translated by Luke)	Clement of Alexandria	ca 155–220	Eusebius, *Ecclesiastical History*, 6.14.3
Unknown	Origen	ca 185–254	Eusebius, *Ecclesiastical History*, 6.14.3
Clement of Rome	Ephraem Syrus	ca 306-373	*Commentarieus in epistolis Pauli nunc primum ex Armenio in Latinum sermonem a partibus Mekhitaristis translati* (Venice 1893).
Luke	Aquinas, T.	1260s	*Commentary on the Epistle to the Hebrews*, trans. by C. Baer (South Bend: St. Augustine's Press, 2006).
Apollos **Unknown**	Luther, M	1545 1522\1546	*Luther's Works*, vol. 8.178; *idem*. vol. 35.394 (Muhlenberg: 1960).
Silas	Boehme, C. F.	1825	*Epistle to the Hebrews* (Leipzig: Barth, 1825).
Peter	Welch, A.	1889	*The Authorship of the Epistle to the Hebrews* (Edinburgh: Oliphant, Anderson and Ferrier, 1889).
Philip	Ramsay, W. M.	1899	"The Date and Authorship of the Epistle to the Hebrews," *The Expositor* 9 (1899): 401-22.

[1] Adapted from Herbert W. Bateman IV, *Charts on the Book of Hebrews* in Kregel Charts of the Bible (Grand Rapid: Kregel, 2012), 17–18.

Priscilla & Aquila (Pricilla dominant)	Harnack, A. von	1900	"Probabilia über die Adresse und den Verfassere des Hebräerbriefs," *ZNTW* 1 (1900): 16–41.
Aristion	Chapman, J.	1905	"Aristion, author of the Epistle to the Hebrews," *RBén* 22 (1905): 50-64.
Stephen	Kirby, V. T.	1923	"The authorship of the Epistle to the Hebrews," *Expository Times* 35 (1923): 375-77.
Barnabus (translated by Luke)	Badcock, F. J.	1937	*The Pauline Epistles and the Epistle to the Hebrews in their Historical Setting* (NY, 1937).
Jude	Dubarle, A. M.	1939	"*Author and Destination of the Epistle to the Hebrews*," *RB* 48 (1939): 506-29.
Voice of Barnabas (written by Luke)	Badcock, F. J.	1937	*The Pauline Epistles and the Epistle to the Hebrews in their Historical Setting* (NY, 1937).
Mary (Mother of Jesus), assisted by Luke and John	Ford, J. M.	1966	"The Mother of Jesus and the Authorship of the Epistle to the Hebrews" *TBT* 82 (1976): 683-94.
Epaphras	Anderson, C. P.	1966	"The Epistle to the Hebrews and the Pauline Letter Collection," *HTR* 59 (1966): 429-438; "Hebrews among the Letters of Paul," *SR* 5 (1975-76): 258-66.
Timothy	Legg, J. D.	1968	"Our Brother Timothy, A Suggested Solution to the Problem of the Authorship of the Epistle to the Hebrews," *EvQ* 40 (1968): 22-23.

3. TO WHOM WAS THE BOOK WRITTEN AND WHEN?

A. Where was the Audience Located?

DEBATED DESTINATIONS FOR THE BOOK HEBREWS[2]

Options	Location	Founding	First Century Ethnicity
Rome	City of Rome: East Bank of the Tiber River, Central Italy	City of Rome: 753 BCE (by Romulus)	Latins, Eutruscans, Greeks, Hellenistic Jews, and others
Jerusalem	City of Jerusalem: Mountains of Judah, Central Judea	City of Jerusalem: 3300 BCE (by Semites: perhaps Jebusites)	Canaanites, Hebrew Jews, Hellenistic Jews, Greeks, Romans, and others.
Antioch Syria	Orontes River in Syria	300 B.C.E. (by Seleucus I)	Native Syrians, Greeks, Cretans, Cypriots, Romans, Hellenistic Jews
Colossea	Lycus River in Phrygia	Prior to 480 B.C.E. (by Pyrigians)	Pryigians, Greeks, Romans, Hellenistic Jews, and others
City of Cyrene	North Africa	630 B.C.E. (by Greeks)	Greeks, Lybians, Romans, Hellenistic Jews, and others

---

[2] Adapted from Herbert W. Bateman IV, *Charts on the Book of Hebrews* in Kregel Charts of the Bible (Grand Rapid: Kregel, 2012), 35.

B. What was their background?

C. What current situation prompted the writing of the book?

D. The Approximate Date?

DEBATED CONSIDERATIONS ABOUT THE DATING[3]

Agreed Upon Considerations = No Debate among Commentators		
Evidence	**Date**	**Explanation**
Jesus' earthly ministry has ended (Hebrews 2:17; 5:7-10; 13:20-21).	29-33	Emphasis throughout Hebrews is upon Jesus' ruling presence in heaven (1:3, 13; 2:28; 4:14; 8:1-6; 10:12).
Clement of Rome is the first to quote Hebrews (1:3, 4, 5, 7, 13; 2:18; 3:1, 2, 5; 6:18; 11:5, 7, 17, 31, 37; 12:1, [6], 9)	95-96	Eighteen quotes are in his 1st Corinth: *1 Clement* 36:2; 36:2; 36.4; 9.4; 36.13; 36.1; 36.1; 12.5; 43.1; 27.2; 9.3; 9:4; 10.7; 12.1; 17.1; 19.2; 56.4; 64.1
Broadest Perimeters for Dating Hebrews = 29 to 96		

Neutral Considerations for Determining Date		
Evidence	**Date**	**Explanation**
Second Generation: The author speaks of certain people having heard the gospel from Jesus (Hebrews 2:3). Does "us" in v. 2 indicate that the author is part of an older (first) generation?	30-70 90s	The two options are inconclusive: For some, the author receives the gospel from Jesus, and he is a first generation believer ("us"). For others, the author is *silent* about his being part of the first generation but views himself ("us") as part of the second generation of saints.
Timothy: Hebrews is written during Timothy's lifetime (Hebrews 13:23). How might the reference of Timothy affect the dating of Hebrews?	50-52 64-68 90s?	Timothy first appears during Paul's second missionary journey (Acts 16:1). If 2 Timothy is Pauline, Timothy is still alive at the time of Paul's death (4:9). Timothy's death an unknown factor.
Neutral considerations appear to narrow the dating of Hebrews = 50s to 90s		

---

[3] Adapted from Herbert W. Bateman IV, *Charts on the Book of Hebrews* in Kregel Charts of the Bible (Grand Rapid: Kregel, 2012), 41–42.

Debated Considerations for Dating		
Evidence	Date	The Debates
Persecution: Hebrews identifies that the readers are experiencing periods of trials (2:18; 4:15), periods of opposition (12:3-4), periods of persecution (10:32-34; 13:3). Determining what the persecution is becomes a determinative factor for dating the book as pre-70.	49 64-68 66-70 81-96	Three options support a **pre-70** dating for Hebrews: Claudius' persecution of the Jew (Acts 18:2; Seutonius, *Life of Claudius* 25.4), • Nero's persecution of Christians (Tert. *AdNat* 1.7.8/9; *Apol* 5.3/4; Eusebus, *Hist* 4.26.9), Jewish Wars (if to Jerusalem Jews) (Jos *Ant* 20.8.9 § 184; *War* 1.1.4§10; 2.14.1§272-76; Tacitus *Ann* 15.44). One option supports a **post-70** dating for Hebrews: Domitian's persecution of Christians (Pliny *Ep* 10.96.1; Eusebus, *Hist* 3.18.4).
Temple: Hebrews is silent about the destruction of Jerusalem's temple. The sacrificial system appears to be in operation (8:4; 9:6–9; 10:1-4; 13:11). The present tense describes the appointment of high priest, Levites priestly office, and service (5:1-4; 7:5; 8:3-4; 10:11; 13:11). The law and the cultic system is presented as coming to an end (7:12; 8:7, 13; 9:10-11; 10:18) Answering the issue about the temple seems to be *most* determinative for a post-70 date.	70 90-96	Two arguments for a **pre-70** date: The shows no awareness about the temple's destruction. In the *Epistle of Barnabas*, while discussing temple practices, the author notes clearly the temple's destruction (16:4). Two arguments for a **post-70** date: While discussing temple practices, Josephus speaks of the temple in the present tense (*Ant* 3.9.5-10.7 § 224-257; *Against Apion* 2.6.77). The author of Hebrews does not discuss the temple, he appeals to the tabernacle (8:5; 9:1-9).
You now, make the call! When was Hebrews written?		

4. HOW IS HEBREWS RELEVANT TODAY?

TRACK THE *CHRIST*-OLOGY

1. INTRODUCTION

2. HOW HEBREWS WORKS

The Structure of the Book of Hebrews
George H. Guthrie

INTRODUCTION: GOD HAS SPOKEN TO US IN A SON (1:1-4)

I. THE POSITION OF THE SON, OUR MESSENGER, IN RELATION TO THE ANGELS (1:5-2:18)

- A. The Son Superior to the Angels (1:5-14) → **Warning:** *Pay Attention to What We Have Heard Through God's Superior Son (2:1-4)*
- ab. The Superior Son, to Whom all things are Submitted, for a Time Became Lower than the Angels (2:5-9)
- B. The Son Lower than the Angels (i.e., among humans) to Suffer for the "sons" (i.e. heirs) (2:10-18)

Jesus, the Supreme Example of a Faithful Son (3:1-6)

The Negative Example of Those Who Did Not Listen to His Voice" (3:7-19)
The Promise of Rest for Those Who Hear His Voice Today (4:1-11)
Warning: *The Power and Effectiveness of God's Word (4:12-13)*

II. THE POSITION OF THE SON, OUR HIGH PRIEST, IN RELATION TO THE EARTHLY SACRIFICIAL SYSTEM (4:14-10:25)

OPENING: HAVING A GREAT HIGH PRIEST, Hold Fast and Draw Near (4:14-16)

NOTICE:

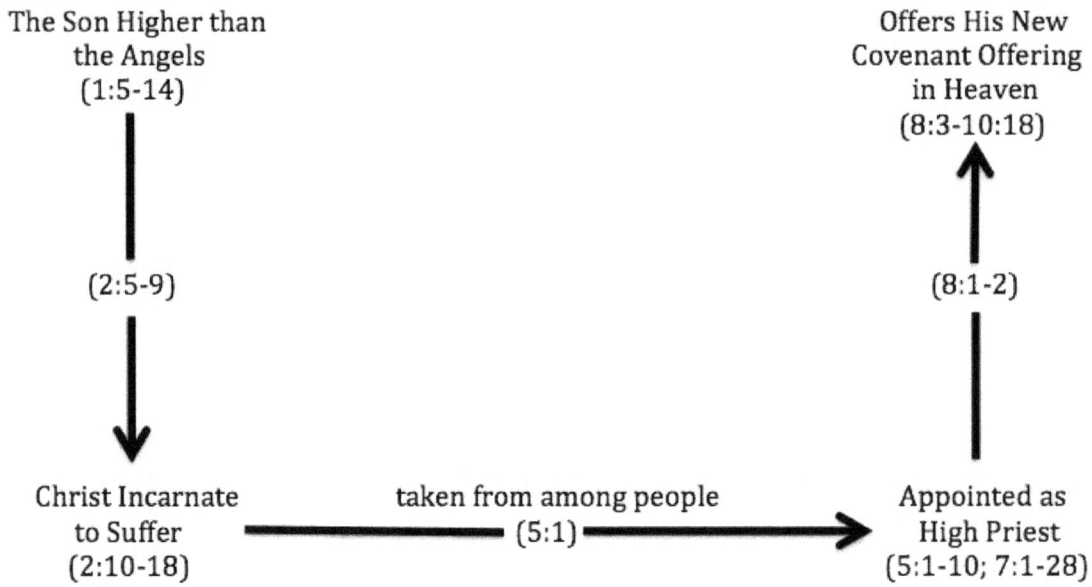

POSITION AND CHARACTER OF JESUS AS REGAL PRIEST IN HEBREWS

Position & Character	Description	Hebrews
Position: Jesus is . . .	seated at the right hand of the throne of God.	1:3 (cp. 8:1); 1:13 (via Ps. 110:1)
	a regal priest after the order of Melchizedek."	5:10; 6:20 5:6; 7:17 (via Ps. 110:4)
	an appointed regal priest by God.	5:5-5 (via Pss. 2:7 & 110:4; cp. 5:1, 4)
	a regal priest exalted above the heavens.	7:26 (cp. 4:14)
	a minister in the heavenly sanctuary.	8:2
	a regal priest of the good things that have come	9:11
Character: Jesus is . . .	a merciful and faithful regal priest.	2:17
	able to help believers who are tempted.	2:18
	able to sympathize with the weaknesses of believers.	4:15
	tempted just like everyday believers, yet without sin.	4:15
	a forerunner of all people who believe (via his regal priesthood).	6:20
	Holy, blameless, unstained, separated from sinners.	7:26
	made perfect forever.	7:28
	securing an eternal redemption for believers.	9:12

OLD TESTAMENT QUOTATIONS IN HEBREWS

Fifty-four out-of three hundred and three verses (18%) contain direct quotations from the Old Testament.

Of these Old Testament citations cited below with English Bible chapter and verse, fifty different quoted verses from the Old Testament occur in the Book of Hebrews.

Quotation	Hebrews	Quotation	Hebrews
Psalm 2:7	1:5	Psalm 110:4	7:17, 21
2 Samuel 7:14	1:5		
Deuteronomy 32:43	1:6	Exodus 25:40	8:5
Psalm 104:4	1:7	Jer. 31:31–34	8:8–12
Psalm 45:5-6	1:8		
Psalm 102:24-26	1:10–12	Exodus 24:8	9:20
Psalm 110:1	1:13		
		Psalm 40:5-7	10:5–9
Psalm 8:3-5	2:6–8	Jeremiah 31:33–34	10:16–17
Psalm 22:22a	2:12	Deuteronomy 32:35	10:30
Isaiah 8:17-18	2:13	Deuteronomy 32:38	
		Psalm 135:14	
Psalm 95:7–11	3:7–11	Habakkuk 2:3–4	10:37–38
Psalm 95:7–8	3:15		
		Genesis 21:12	11:18
Psalm 95:11	4:3, 5		
Genesis 2:2	4:4	Proverbs 3:11–12	12:5–6
Psalm 95:7–8	4:7	Exodus 19:12–13	12:20
		Deuteronomy 9:19	12:21
Psalm 2:7	5:5	Haggai 2:6	12:26
Psalm 110:4	5:6	Deuteronomy 4:24	12:29
		Deuteronomy 31:6	
Genesis 22:17	6:14	Psalm 118:6	13:5
			13:6

3. FOUR MAIN MOVEMENTS OF HEBREWS' *CHRIST*-OLOGY

A. JESUS IS _____ THAN YOU EVER IMAGINED

HEBREWS 1:5–14

⁵For to which of the angels did God ever say,
  "You are my Son, today I have begotten you"?
Or again,
  "I will be to him a father, and he shall be to me a son"?
⁶And again, when he brings the firstborn into the world, he says,
  "Let all God's angels worship him."
⁷Of the angels he says,
  "He makes his angels winds, and his ministers a flame of fire."
⁸But of the Son he says,
  "Your throne, O God, is forever and ever, the scepter of uprightness is the scepter of your kingdom.
   ⁹You have loved righteousness and hated wickedness; therefore God, your God, has anointed you with the oil of gladness beyond your companions."
¹⁰And,
  "You, Lord, laid the foundation of the earth in the beginning,
    and the heavens are the work of your hands;
      ¹¹they will perish, but you remain;
      they will all wear out like a garment, ¹²like a robe you will roll them up, like a garment they will be changed.
  But you are the same, and your years will have no end."
¹³And to which of the angels has he ever said,
  "Sit at my right hand until I make your enemies a footstool for your feet"?
¹⁴Are they not all ministering spirits sent out to serve for the sake of those who are to inherit salvation? (ESV)

B. JESUS IS MORE _____ THAN YOU EVER THOUGHT

Hebrews 2:10–18

¹⁰For it was fitting that he, for whom and by whom all things exist, in bringing many sons to glory, should make the founder of their salvation perfect through suffering. ¹¹For he who sanctifies and those who are sanctified all have one source. That is why he is not ashamed to call them brothers,
¹²saying,

> "I will tell of your name to my brothers;
> in the midst of the congregation I will sing your praise."

¹³And again,

> "I will put my trust in him."

And again,

> "Behold, I and the children God has given me."

¹⁴Since therefore the children share in flesh and blood, he himself likewise partook of the same things, that through death he might destroy the one who has the power of death, that is, the devil, ¹⁵and deliver all those who ˡthrough fear of death were subject to lifelong slavery. ¹⁶For surely it is not angels that he helps, but he ᵐhelps the offspring of Abraham. ¹⁷Therefore he had to be made like his brothers in every respect, so that he might become a merciful and faithful high priest in the service of God, to make propitiation for the sins of the people. ¹⁸For because he himself has suffered when tempted, he is able to help those who are being tempted. (ESV)

Let's Know the Bible Conference: Hebrews

C. JESUS BRINGS YOU _____ THAN YOU EVER DREAMED POSSIBLE (5:1-7:28)

HEBREWS 5:1–10

¹For every high priest chosen from among men is appointed to act on behalf of men in relation to God, to offer gifts and sacrifices for sins. ²He can deal gently with the ignorant and wayward, since he himself is beset with weakness. ³Because of this he is obligated to offer sacrifice for his own sins just as he does for those of the people. ⁴And no one takes this honor for himself, but only when called by God, just as Aaron was.

⁵So also Christ did not exalt himself to be made a high priest, but was appointed by him who said to him,
    "You are my Son, today I have begotten you";
⁶as he says also in another place,
    "You are a priest forever, after the order of Melchizedek."

⁷In the days of his flesh, Jesus offered up prayers and supplications, with loud cries and tears, to him who was able to save him from death, and he was heard because of his reverence. ⁸Although he was a son, he learned obedience through what he suffered. ⁹And being made perfect, he became the source of eternal salvation to all who obey him, ¹⁰being designated by God a high priest after the order of Melchizedek. (ESV)

HEBREWS 6:15–20

¹⁵And thus Abraham, having patiently waited, obtained the promise. ¹⁶For people swear by something greater than themselves, and in all their disputes an oath is final for confirmation. ¹⁷So when God desired to show more convincingly to the heirs of the promise the unchangeable character of his purpose, he guaranteed it with an oath, ¹⁸so that by two unchangeable things, in which it is impossible for God to lie, we who have fled for refuge might have strong encouragement to hold fast to the hope set before us. ¹⁹We have this as a sure and steadfast anchor of the soul, a hope that enters into the inner place behind the curtain, ²⁰where Jesus has gone as a forerunner on our behalf, having become a high priest forever after the order of Melchizedek. (ESV)

D. JESUS IS MORE _____ THAN YOU DARED HOPE (8:3-10:18)

Hebrews 10:11–18

¹¹And every priest stands daily at his service, offering repeatedly the same sacrifices, which can never take away sins. ¹²But when Christ had offered for all time a single sacrifice for sins, he sat down at the right hand of God, ¹³waiting from that time until his enemies should be made a footstool for his feet. ¹⁴For by a single offering he has perfected for all time those who are being sanctified.

¹⁵And the Holy Spirit also bears witness to us; for after saying, ¹⁶"This is the covenant that I will make with them after those days, declares the Lord: I will put my laws on their hearts, and write them on their minds," ¹⁷then he adds, "I will remember their sins and their lawless deeds no more." ¹⁸Where there is forgiveness of these, there is no longer any offering for sin. (ESV)

CONCLUSION:

HEAR THE WORD OF ENCOURAGEMENT

1. INTRODUCTION

HUCK & JIM -

2. HOW HEBREWS WORKS (WITH EXHORTATION)

   A. The Exhortation Material Works by _____ .

B. The Exhortation Material Has a Key Message:

GOD HAS SPOKEN BY HIS SON;

_____ ***THE PROMISES,***

HEED THE _____ .

C. The Exhortation Material Uses Various Approaches:

1) Promises & _____ .

2) Deep Theology & _____ .

3) Positive and Negative _____ .

THE DANGERS OF APOSTASY IN HEBREWS[1]

Types of Dangers	Brief Description of the Danger	Occurrence in Hebrews
Passive Dangers	Believers are encouraged not to drift away or lose sight of the message.	2:1
	Believers are encouraged not to neglect the message.	2:3
	Believers are encouraged not to fall short of the goal.	4:1
	Believers are encouraged not to lose hold of their confession.	4:14
	Believers are encouraged not to become dull in their understanding of the message.	5:11
	Believers are encouraged not to become sluggish in learning more about the message.	6:12 (cp. 5:12-14)
	Believers are encouraged not to lose their confidence.	10:19, 23
	Believers are encouraged not to lose heart.	12:3
	Believers are encouraged not to be carried away by strange teachings.	13:9
Active Dangers	Believers will develop a sinful, unbelieving heart that will turn away from the living God.	3:12
	Believers will exhibit disobedience that mirrors the Kadesh Bernea community.	4:11
	Believers will fall away from Jesus and hold him in contempt.	6:6
	Believers will neglect to meet together.	10:25
	Believers will persist, willfully, in sin and profane the blood of Jesus.	10:26
	Believers will reject God who speaks from heaven.	12:25
External Dangers	Believers will fall away due to the assaults that test their faith.	2:18; 4:16
	Believers will turn away due to their suffering through persecution.	10:32-34; 12:4
	Believers will reject the message due to the threat of torture and imprisonment.	10:33-34; 13:3
	Believers may forfeit future restoration or opportunity for a second repentance.	3:19; 6:4-8; 10:26-31; 12:16-17

[1] Adapted from Herbert W. Bateman IV, *Charts on the Book of Hebrews* in Kregel Charts of the Bible (Grand Rapid: Kregel, 2012), 145.

VIEWS ON THE WARNING PASSAGES IN HEBREWS[2]

Commentator	Source	Suggested Divisions
Bruce, F.F.	*Exploring Hebrews: An Expository Commentary* in The John Phillips Commentary Series. Grand Rapids: Kregel, revised edition, 1977, 1988 (pp. 12-14).	Admonition #1 = 2:1-4 Admonition #2 = 3:7-19 Admonition #3 = 5:11-14 Admonition #4 = 10:26-31 Pay Heed = 12:25-29
Guthrie, George H.	*The Structure of Hebrews: A Text-Linguistic Analysis.* Grand Rapids: Baker, 1998 (p. 135).	Warning #1 = 2:1-4 Warning #2 = 4:12-13 Warning #3 = 6:4-8 Warning #4 = 10:26-31 Warning #5 = 12:25-29
Koester, Craig R.	*Hebrews* in The Anchor Bible. New York: Doubleday, 2001 (pp. 84-85).	Warning/Encouragement #1 = 5:11-6:20 Warning/Encouragement #2 = 10:26-39 Warning/Encouragement #3 = 12:25-27
Lane, William L.	*Hebrews 1-8* in Word Biblical Commentary. Waco, TX: Word, 1991 (pp. 33, 80, 128). *Hebrews 9-13* in Word Biblical Commentary. Waco, TX: Word, 1991 (pp. 271, 435).	Warning #1 = 2:1-4 Warning #2 = 3:7-19 Warning #3 = 5:11-6:12 Warning #4 = 10:19-39 Warning #5 = 12:12-29
Phillips, John.	*Exploring Hebrews: An Expository Commentary* in The John Phillips Commentary Series. Grand Rapids: Kregel, revised edition, 1977, 1988 (pp. 12-14).	Warning #1 = 2:1-4 Warning #2 = 3:7-4:13 Warning #3 = 5:11-6:20 Warning #4 = 10:26-39 Warning #5 = 12:15-29
Bateman, Herbert W.	*Four Views on the Warning Passages in Hebrews* Grand Rapids: Kregel, 2007 (p. 27)	Warning #1 = 2:1-4 Warning #2 = 3:7-4:13 Warning #3 = 5:11-6:20 Warning #4 = 10:26-39 Warning #5 = 12:15-29

---

[2] Adapted from Herbert W. Bateman IV, *Charts on the Book of Hebrews* in Kregel Charts of the Bible (Grand Rapid: Kregel, 2012), 149.

3. TWO EXAMPLES OF WARNING PASSAGES

A. Hebrews 3:6,14

> HEBREWS 3:6
>
> But Christ is faithful as a Son over His house. And we are his house, ***if we hold onto*** the confidence and the boast of our hope.
>
> HEBREWS 3:14
>
> For we have become companions of the Messiah ***if we hold onto*** the commitment that we had at the beginning firmly until the end

1) A Few Key Terms

2) Is He Speaking to Believers?

Let's Know the Bible Conference: Hebrews 46

3) What is the Logic of These Verses (and the Ministry Backdrop)?

A statement of _____,

followed by a _____.

- You, however, are controlled not by the sinful nature but by the Spirit, if the Spirit of God lives in you. (Romans 8:9)
- If we are children, then we are heirs—heirs of God and co-heirs with Christ, if indeed we share in his sufferings in order that we may also share in his glory. (Romans 8:17)
- Behold then the kindness and severity of God; to those who fell, severity, but to you, God's kindness, if you continue in his kindness; (Romans 11:22)
- Do you not realize that Christ Jesus is in you—unless, of course, you fail the test . . . (2 Corinthians 13:5b)
- **ALL HAVE TO DO WITH A PERSON'S RELATIONSHIP WITH GOD!**

4) So What is Going On Here?

5) Application: The Practical Payoff?

Let's Know the Bible Conference: Hebrews

B. Hebrews 6:4–6

⁴For it is impossible, in the case of those who have once been enlightened, who have tasted the heavenly gift, and have shared in the Holy Spirit, ⁵and have tasted the goodness of the word of God and the powers of the age to come, ⁶and then have fallen away, to restore them again to repentance, since they are crucifying once again the Son of God to their own harm and holding him up to contempt.

1) The Purpose and Process?

2) Key Images from the _____ Wanderings

3) "Shaming" and "Crucifying"?

4) Different Interpretations of this Passage?

- Hypothetical Situation –

- Non-Christian Jews –

- Covenant community view –

- Back-slider Believers –

- "Repentance of God" –

- Christians who lose their salvation –

- People who manifest they are not true Christians

5) Application: Hebrews 6:4-6 in Ministry Today

- Many struggle with this passage –

- Don't give people assurance they shouldn't have –

- There is a difference between regeneration and participation - (people join for various reasons) –

- Encourage to look to Jesus and the gospel –

Conclusion:

Practical Christian Resources

Trained in the Fear of God
Randy Stimson
978-0-8254-3907-0 • $26.99

Sexual Intimacy in Marriage, 3rd Edition
Dr. William Cutrer and Sandra Glahn
978-0-8254-2437-3 • $14.99

Wounded Women of the Bible
Dena Dyer
978-0-8254-4214-8 • $12.99

Love Letters from the Edge
Shelly Beach and Wanda Sanchez
978-0-8254-4347-3 • $15.99

Hope After Betrayal
Meg Wilson
978-0-8254-3935-3 • $10.99

Foundations of Christian Thought
Mark P. Cosgrove
978-0-8254-2434-2 • $15.99

BUILDING CONFIDENCE IN READING THE BIBLE

HERBERT W. BATEMAN IV
LEE COMPSON
AARON HOAK
MICHAEL HONTZ
AARON C. PEER
TIMOTHY D. SPRANKLE
JEREMY WIKE

BUILDING CONFIDENCE

THE CYBER–CENTER FOR BIBLICAL STUDIES posts monthly blogs authored by pastors in Northern Indiana under the direction of Timothy D. Sprankle, Senior Pastor of Leesburg Grace Brethren Church.

The monthly blogs are posted on the Cyber-Center for Biblical Studies website: hwbateman.com as well as the Let's Know the Bible Conference FaceBook page: facebook.com/KnowTheBibleConference.

The following is a collected assortment of those blogs, interspersed with a few devotional thoughts from a forthcoming Kerux commentary on Hebrews.

READ A GOOD TRANSLATION

by Aaron C. Peer

Senior Pastor of Charter Oak Community Church

What translation a believer should use is often a touchy subject in churches. Let's think this through carefully. I want to start with a foundational point. *Every translation is an interpretation of the text.* Translators have to address many issues before he or she even begins the process. English translation reflects thousands of choices that a team of scholars has made on your behalf. This interpretation is unavoidable. These choices are necessary because we are separated from the world of the Bible not only in its original language, but also its culture, time, and geography. Therefore, some interpretive work needs to be done to communicate across these barriers

Generally speaking, translators choose from one of three different philosophies. Each one has a different opinion on how many of interpretative choices they should make for the reader.

The first philosophy is **formal equivalence**. Such translations try to get *as close as possible to the original*, making *as few choices as possible*. These translations are often called **word-for-word** translations. The KJV, NAS, and more recently the ESV are examples of this type of translation. They seek to use similar words and grammatical constructions, interpreting just enough to make the text understandable in English. This philosophy puts a substantial amount of faith in the reader. Translators believe the reader should bridge the gap and make the choices rather than the translator. For instance, the KJV says that Adam knew his wife Eve. Someone who knows the original setting of the Bible knows that this is a euphemism for sexual relations, but the original meaning might be lost on a new believer. Therefore, this type of translation is good for someone who knows the ancient world fairly well.

The second philosophy is **dynamic equivalence**. These translations attempt to put the *original meaning* of the text into *understandable language*. These translations are often called **meaning-for-meaning** translations. The NIV and the TNIV are examples of this philosophy. They attempt to bridge the gap, while still retaining many words and phrases from the original. The interpretive choices make the translation more removed from the exact wording of the text, but also make it easier to read and understand. Therefore, this type of translation is good for reading in public or just for devotional reading.

The final philosophy is **paraphrase** or **free translation**. These translations try to *eliminate the need for readers to make choices at all*. These translations are often called **paragraph-for-paragraph** translations. The Message and the Living Bible are examples. This type of translation is good for non-believers who have no biblical background or believers who don't know the ancient world very well. It can also be a fresh perspective for more mature or knowledgeable believers as well. Basically, free translations end up being very readable and vibrant commentaries on the text.

So back to our original question: *Which translation should we use?* Well, they all have their value. Your reason and circumstance may serve as the best guide to choosing. If you are studying deeply, maybe the ESV or the NAS is best. If you are reading or reciting the text in public or just want to casually read it in devotions, the NIV would be a good option. And if you are looking for a fresh perspective or are handing a Bible to a non-believer or new Christian, perhaps the Message would be a good choice. In any case, what is most important is that you read the Bible.

© March 15, 2016

GRASP GOD'S BIG PICTURE

by Lee Compson

Senior Pastor of Milford First Brethren Church

Open up Scripture to any number of passages and you are likely to find yourself mired in different types of literature or categories of communication. There are sweeping narrative stories. There are ornately crafted poems. There are carefully worded law codes and terrifyingly intense visions.

So how are we to make sense of such diversity?

We must grasp God's Big Picture. From beginning to end, the Bible cohesively traces God's plan for all of history, starting in Genesis with the very creation of the world and concluding with Revelation.

The entire first portion of the Bible – the Old Testament – traces the work of God over vast periods of time. He created the universe perfectly, including mankind. But Scripture describes how quickly humanity corrupted God's creation through disobedience and sin. Yet hope did not vanish. God began working to redeem mankind from their fall. He chose the nation of Israel, starting with Abraham, as the instrument through which he would save a people for himself. He made covenants—with Abraham, Moses, David, and the New—both to govern his people and to confirm his gracious purposes for them.

As time wore on, it became obvious that Israel could not live up to her end of the covenants. So God followed through with refining judgment, as communicating through his prophets. Meanwhile, promises of a coming Deliverer, God's Messiah who would make all things right, remained unfulfilled.

The New Testament demonstrates that this redemptive promise was fulfilled when God sent Jesus to be that promised Messiah. The Gospels record much of Jesus' life and teachings, along with his sacrificial death and supernatural resurrection. It is his death and resurrection that sparked a new movement, the Church. The rest of the New Testament—the Acts narrative and apostolic letters—focuses on the formation of this new people of God. As the canon comes to a close, the book of Revelation acts as the capstone to God's Big Picture, by casting a glorious vision of the future that awaits God's faithful followers.

While God intervened in different ways at different times throughout history, it is vital that we understand the progression of His work. The different types of literature within the Bible certainly require their own specific rules. Yet in each of these genres, it's crucial to understand their context and position within God's Big Picture. The better we understand God's Big Picture, the better we will be able to handle his Word and discern his will for us today.

© February 15, 2016

JESUS, GOD'S "DIFFERENT" PRIEST (HEBREWS 7:11)

by Herbert W. Bateman IV

President of the Cyber-Center for Biblical Studies

So if perfection had in fact been possible through the Levitical priesthood—for on that basis the people received the law—what further need would there have been for a different priest to arise, said to be in the order of Melchizedek and not in Aaron's order?

Before I share some thoughts about Hebrews 7:11, let me say something first about Hebrews chapter seven.

Hebrews 7 highlights the author's central teaching about a man named Melchizedek and how it is that Jesus resembles Melchizedek, particularly his royal priesthood. The author first retells and interprets a story about Melchizedek found in Genesis 14:18–20 (verses 1–10). He then turns his interpretation into an application about God changing the Levitical priesthood and terminating the Mosaic Law (verses 11–19). He concludes the chapter by way of three contrasts between the priests from the tribe of Levi and Jesus whose priesthood is like Melchizedek's (verses 20–28).

Now when I first read Hebrews 7:11 above, I said to myself, "What?" Yet it helped when I finally realized that the author wrote a sentence that presented a contrary-to-fact or an unreal condition. Here's what I mean. Let me rewrite the verse this way: "If perfection had in fact been possible through the Levitical priesthood" (but it is not), "would there have been a need for another priest to arise" (but there was). So the author tells us two things: (1) the Levitical priesthood did not bring perfection and (2) there was a need for a different kind of priest.

Now a Levitical priest was a priest whose ancestry could be traced back to Levi, a son of Jacob (see Genesis 24:34; Exodus 28:41). Even though they did not have "ancestry.com," they knew their ancestry. Moses and his brother Aaron were also Levites. Yet not everyone who was born a Levite entered the priesthood. Unlike his father Zachariah who served as a priest, John the Baptist was not a priest (see Luke 1:5, 8–9; 2:59–80). So a Levitical priest was someone who could trace their ancestry back to Levi and who were eligible to enter the priesthood (like Zachariah) and perform priestly duties.

We also need to define the word "perfection" (τελείωσις). "Perfection" does not mean faultless or to be "without flaws." "Perfection" in Hebrews concerns a person's relationship with God. So the author tells us that Levitical priests, no matter what they did, no matter how many sacrifices the offered, no matter how many prayers they prayed, Levitical priests were unable to fix or establish a person's relationship with God. So the author tells us there was need. There was a need for a "different" priest.

The word "different" (ἕτερον) is rather significant here because the author chose "different" over the word that meant "another" (ἄλλος). The word "another" meant another of the "same kind" of Levitical priest. Yet for the author of Hebrews, there was a need for a "different kind" of priest. The different kind of priest that was needed was a royal priest similar to that of Melchizedek and not a man from Aaron's lineage. So a notable change in priesthoods was necessary to fix a person's relationship with God.

So whom does God rise up to fix this problem? Jesus! Jesus was not a descendant from Levi. He was a descendant of Judah (Levi's brother; see Genesis 29:35; 49:10). Jesus' ancestry could also be traced back to King David (see Matthew 1:6–16). Hebrews tells us that Jesus was that different kind of priest to "arise" and fix the relational problem that exists between God and people. And just like Melchizedek who was a royal priest, Jesus is God's appointed royal priest who has made it possible for me to have a relationship with God for which I am truly grateful.

© February 10, 2016

READ, RE-READ, AND READ AGAIN TO BUILD CONFIDENCE

by Timothy D. Sprankle

Senior Pastor of Leesburg Grace Brethren Church

For two years, I participated in Life Transformation Groups, a simple but powerful mode of biblical accountability. LTGs comprise a few people of the same gender, meeting weekly to share God's work and word. Members of an LTG are expected to read thirty chapters of the Bible between meetings.

In case you missed it, I repeat: members of an Life Transformation Groups are expected to read **thirty chapters** a week.

Life Transformation Groups assume the transformative power of Scripture and accept no shortcuts in the formation process. They may not suit the legalist or lethargic believer, but for the typical follower of Jesus, they provide a social incentive to read God's word. As further incentive, Life Transformation Groups include this caveat: *If a single member of the group fails to read the target number* (I repeat: thirty chapters), *everyone sticks with the same assignment the following week.*

Life Transformation Groups do not come with a ready-made reading guide; each group selects its **thirty chapters** and gets to work. Members may read thirty consecutive chapters or repeat smaller sections to reach the mark. Missing the chapter goal may lead to another ten cycles through the Sermon on the Mount or another long haul through Exodus.

Life Transformation Groups granted me numerous opportunities to read, re-read, and read parts of the Bible again. I once read the book of Galatians *five times a week* for *six weeks straight*! The apostle Paul's voice was lodged in my head screaming "*anathema*" (1:8) to my accountability partner who kept missing our target.

In an age where biblical literacy has given way to verse-of-the-day expediency, confidence in God's word suffers. A commitment akin to the Life Transformation Groups reprioritizes reading (and re-reading) the Bible. *The process of reading, re-reading, and reading again the same portion of Scripture builds biblical confidence by unveiling new observations and encouraging reflection.*

Repetition unveils new observations. Reading (and re-reading) Philippians will surface key words and themes we did not notice on the first run through. Or, perhaps, a third trek through Acts showcases the extensive role women play in the early church. And I am certain after the sixth reading of Haggai we will finally master the book's literary flow. Irony, allusions, and other literary devices we miss during our first few readings will eventually stand out. We gain new insights when we read, re-read, and read again.

Repetition leads to reflection. Of course, every reader is guilty of glossing over certain words and sentences, numbed by familiarity. In the short-term, repetition can breed contempt. However in the long-term, repetition builds muscle memory. Repetition lodges a text in our minds so we cannot help but hear it in our music, see it on our screens, recall it in our crises, and apply it in our lives. After thirty cycles through Galatians, I witnessed fruit of the spirit at every turn. We embody the Scriptures when we read, re-read, and read them again.

God's Word—so rich and so deep—invites multiple readings. Forming a Life Transformation Groups is not a prerequisite for reading, re-reading, and reading again. So pick a book, a goal, and get started.

© May 15, 2017

READ THE BIBLE IN BIG CHUNKS

by Michael Hontz

Senior Pastor of Pleasant View Bible Church

"If you could give just one piece of advice on how to get more out of my Bible study, what would it be?" I've been asked this question many times over the years. My answer today is quite different than it would have been during my earliest years in ministry. Perhaps it is surprising.

To get more out of Bible study, read Scripture in larger chunks and look for the theme(s) that hold the book together.

If you're like me, you were taught to slow down and consider each word, maybe even look in Greek or Hebrew lexicons to maximize your study. While this can certainly be helpful, I've found it can also be a detriment to grasping the broader context. I would suggest first reading through an entire book of the Bible in one sitting. Longer books of the Bible (e.g., Genesis, Exodus) aren't as difficult to read through in one sitting as you might think. They require two and half to three hours; however, since most people don't have that much time to read in one day, reading a larger book in a week is more achievable.

After the initial reading, repeat the process for several days or weeks, depending on the size of the book. Repeated reading of the same book deepens understanding and appreciation. You will be amazed at the things you will notice your third and fourth times through that you previously missed. Additionally, you will begin to see literary themes that create connections between otherwise disconnected sections of the book.

When I first read Exodus in this way, I noticed how the theme of worship dominates the book. In chapters 3-10, Moses tells Pharaoh almost a dozen times to let God's people go so they can worship God. Exodus fifteen comprises a worship song about God's salvation. Four of the Ten Commandments deal directly with worship. Later portions of the book describe the tabernacle and its furnishings, as well as the priesthood and their ministry, all of which define Israelite worship for centuries to come. In chapter thirty-two, worship of the golden calf contrasts the pure form that should typify a believer. When one realizes how worship dominates the book, it isn't hard to see how other stories, such as Moses gazing on and reflecting the glory of God, fit naturally within this broader theme as well.

For me, seeing these sorts of themes tie together a book like Exodus adds value to the focused study of a single word or couple of sentences. Actually, because of my focus on this broader theme, I discovered that the word translated "worship" or "serve" in regards to God's calling his people out of Egypt (3:12, 4:23, 7:16, etc.) is the same Hebrew term translated "work" or "serve" in context of the Israelites' service of

Pharaoh (1:14, 5:9, 18, etc.) which is itself a pretty interesting literary foil, but that's another article for another day.

© January 15, 2017

READ THE BIBLE WITH OTHERS

by Lee Compson

Senior Pastor at Milford First Brethren Church

One of my favorite classes in college focused on C.S. Lewis' writings. I was familiar with his famous works, but wasn't ready for the immersion this course would provide. The imagination and symbolism of many of his writings proved difficult to keep up with. Thus each class session became critical because our professor emphasized group discussion as we processed the latest reading. The class dynamic always stimulated and helped piece together Lewis's stories.

I realize many Christians have a similar experience with the Bible. Even long time churchgoers sometimes feel inadequate when reading and trying to understand the Bible for themselves. While the Bible applies to our modern lives, it is filled with strange terms, strange names, and strange stories that can sidetrack us from fully grasping the message. And though a good study Bible may offer helpful notes, even they can interrupt the flow of reading through a passage.

To overcome these difficulties, reading the Bible with others offers meaningful insights. This can be done in two ways and will boost our confidence in knowing and applying God's Word.

1. Reading **with** others: By this I mean reading the same passages on a planned schedule with others. A small discipleship or accountability group can follow a reading plan where all read identical passages during the week and come back to share what they learned.

2. Reading *alongside* others: This approach involves the basic reading aloud of a passage within a small group or Sunday School. Not all people are extremely adept at reading hard names and words, but having different voices and styles can actually bring out more of the text than if just one person does all the reading. Scripture was intended to be read aloud and heard, and there are aspects of God's Word that are missed if they are only read silently.

In the end, group efforts can boost our confidence in handling God's Word in at least three ways.

1. <u>Different perspectives can enrich our understanding of the text</u>. When we study

the Bible in groups, diversity will emerge that benefits all involved. Different people of different genders and different experiences will read passages differently. Those unique observations can help highlight more truth, especially in a context where questions and insights are welcomed.

2. <u>Tricky concepts are better handled in community</u>. Bible studies can be fertile ground for ignorance or mediocre interpretations. However, the "two heads are better than one" principle still applies. When hard issues and questions rise out of the text, it's better to have more resources at your disposal than just your own limited viewpoint.

3. <u>It takes the pressure off</u>. Every so often, I hear people express embarrassment that "I should know that," feeling inadequate about their basic knowledge of the faith. Studying the Bible within a group setting can be a "rising tides lift all ships" situation, where we all benefit from each other's contributions.

Let me put in one final word about this idea. We have created the ***Let's Know the Bible Conference*** for this very issue. We desire to build people's confidence in their Bible knowledge and application one book at a time. We hope you will attend this year's event as we seek to be equipped to better handle the book of Hebrews.

© March 8, 2017

READ THE BIBLE AS A FAMILY

by Jeremy Wike

Senior Pastor Community of Hope Grace Brethren Church

Certain growth stages of children are predictable. One of my favorites, in my limited journey of fatherhood, is the "Why?" phase. By the age of three, children follow everything a parent says with "Why?" Curiosity in children is both delightful and terrifying.

We want our children to absorb all they can about life, but there's always the chance they will ask risky questions—the kind where answers are too complicated, too delicate, or, let's face it, too revealing of our own ignorance. I wonder if this fear of being caught without a good answer contributes to why many parents don't make family Bible reading more of a priority.

Can I confess something to you if you promise not to tell my four kids? (I have a reputation as a pastor to protect, you know.) Okay. Here goes: *I still have lots of questions about the Bible.* And sometimes I mispronounce names and places. And I still want to tell God that He could have been nicer to Lot's wife. And to Job. Is that okay with God?

I wonder if God is more interested in our engagement with His story than He is that we confidently have answers to our kids' humdinger questions. I wonder if God simply wants us to be committed to the journey of knowing Him through His Word and allowing His Spirit to teach us—parents and children alike. I wonder if our kids will thank us as adults for acknowledging that God allows tension and questions that we can't reconcile. If these are true, then allow me to offer three benefits to habitually reading the Bible with our families, no matter their ages or our (lack of?) Bible literacy:

1. **God wants us to see Himself** as He acts out His love and justice through history. In other words, we learn about God *in action* throughout the Bible. Our kids need to see that God isn't aloof, isn't wringing His hands at the world's problems, and isn't a haphazard tyrant. He responds *differently* throughout history, but He's still the Sovereign, Personal God of Scripture.

2. **God wants us to see our need for His love and grace** reaching its climax on the cross where Jesus bore the weight of the sin of the world. But we must not overlook that his love and grace are present from beginning to end of His story.

3. **God wants us to see that He uses His people to shine the light of Jesus into our topsy-turvy world**. Instead of waiting for God to get angry and smite the "enemy", God's M.O. is to call ordinary people—like you and me—to insert ourselves into the messes of the world and act on His behalf. That hasn't changed since God called the likes of Noah, Gideon, Jonah, Daniel, Nehemiah, Esther, and Peter.

Begin your journey of family devotions by grabbing one of many great kids' Bibles available and get reading. Otherwise, you may hear your children later asking you: *"Why didn't you help me understand the Bible better when I was younger?"*

© June 15, 2016

JESUS, OUR ETERNAL INTERCESSOR (HEBREWS 7:25)

by Herbert W. Bateman IV

President of the Cyber-Center for Biblical Studies

So he is able to save for all time those who come to God through him, because he always lives to intercede for them.

As mentioned above, Hebrews 7 highlights the author's central teaching about a man named Melchizedek and how Jesus resembles Melchizedek's royal priesthood. The author retells and interprets a story about Melchizedek (verses 1–10). Applies God's changing of the Levitical priesthood and terminating the Mosaic Law (verses 11–19). And he concludes with three contrasts between the priests from the tribe of Levi and Jesus whose priesthood is like Melchizedek's (verses 20–28). Naturally, verse 25 appears in the third contrast.

Hebrews 7:25 provides the implications (ὅθεν) for the contrast with special attention given to the duration between Levitical priests and Jesus spoken of in verses 23–24. In essence, verse 25 answers: So what? What's the big deal about the duration of Jesus as our royal priest versus a Levitical priest? Verse 25 reads, "So he is able to save for all time those who come to God through him, because he always lives to intercede for them."

Two rather significant implications appear here. First, Jesus "is able to save." This ability is not a mere possibility. It is a certainty (cf. 2:18; 4:15; 5:7). Naturally, the verb "to save" (σῴζειν) could refer to either a person's physical deliverance or spiritual deliverance. A navy seal might save or rescue a reporter from an outrageous Isis incarceration. That would be an example of physical deliverance. Yet here "to save" speaks of a person's spiritual deliverance, namely to experience the complete forgiveness of any and all our wrong doings before God (intentional and unintentional; cf. 2:3).

Second, our spiritual deliverance has an unlimited duration. It is "forever" (εἰς τὸ παντελές). Yet some say it means "completely" (as in KJV ESV NIV translations) or "for all time" (as in NASB NRSV NLT translations). On the hand, "completely" suggests the degree to which Jesus saves an individual. It is thorough. On the other hand, "for all time" suggests an unlimited duration. His ability to provide spiritual deliverance is for all eternity. The latter view seems best because it is in keeping with Jesus endlessness (v 16) and eternality (v 17). The point: people no longer approach God through a Levitical priest whose role is limited due to their inevitable death that terminates his priesthood but rather through God's resurrected eternal royal priest, Jesus (cf. John 14:6–7; 1 John 4:23; 5:1). This raises a question: Why? Why is this eternal duration of Jesus' royal priesthood such a big deal?

The last statement in verse 25 tells us why: "because he always lives to intercede for them." Jesus lives. Jesus is immortal. The expressed purpose of this eternality is to make "intercession" (ἐντυγχάνειν) on behalf of all those who follow him. Whenever "intercession" is used with "for" or "on behalf of" (ὑπέρ), it carries an important message. In Romans 8:34, Jesus "intercedes on behalf of us" therefore no one can bring a charge against those who follow Jesus. Here in verse 25, Jesus as the royal high priest "intercedes on behalf of" those all those who come to God through him (7:25a).

What has been encouraging to me is that Jesus' intercedes continual for me (and I really need a person to state my case before God because I fail him daily). Unfortunately, this theological concept of intercession has been "grotesquely misrepresented in popular

Christian thought." One commentator puts it this way, "He (= Jesus) is not to be thought of 'as an ornate, standing ever before the Father with outstretched arms, like the figures in the mosaics of the catacombs, and with strong crying and tears pleading our cause in the presence of a reluctant God; but as an *enthroned* Priest-King, asking what He will from a Father who always hears and grants His request." This reminds me of words in a song: "King Jesus is all, my all in all. I know that he answers, me when I call. Walking by my side, he satisfies. King Jesus is all. My all and all."

© February 17, 2016

INCREASING A CONGREGATION'S BIBLE KNOWLEDGE

by Timothy D. Sprankle

Senior Pastor of Leesburg Grace Brethren Church

My daughter asked me the other day if she could underline in her Bible. I said an emphatic, "Yes."

Unprompted, she added, "Samuel is my favorite book. I like reading about David." And I liked hearing that she likes reading.

Claire is ten, and a year ago I weaned her and her sister Margot off picture bibles to the actual text. I started reading through the gospel of Mark with them to give them a ground floor picture of Jesus. They already knew he was mighty and divine. Now they're seeing he is enigmatic, secretive, and purposeful. They ask far more questions now, not only to extend their bedtime, but also because the Scriptures have piqued their imagination.

I want the Word of God to captivate my children. I want their Bibles filled with personal notes, highlights, and bookmarks. I want them to understand the text.

Biblical literacy stands near the top of my list of qualities I desire for all believers—eight-year old children and eighty-year old congregants. However, as most Christians have discovered, biblical literacy does not come easily. Sometimes it's a Bible problem: the text is confusing, complex, or boring. Sometimes it's an Us problem: we are busy, tired, or undisciplined.

Biblical literacy comes when we overcome both personal obstacles and lack of understanding.
To overcome personal obstacles, it helps to have a reading plan and accountability. The plan should include when you will read, where you will read, and how much you plan to read. A journal may be helpful for tracking thoughts and keeping them on track. But do not confuse a plan for a law: a reading plan should to prompt us, not shame us.

Fortunately, we live in an age where resources for understanding abound. Great sermons and articles flood the Internet. Study Bibles and reading guides give practical helps. As a pastor, I provide weekly exhortation in my sermons, boosted by classroom materials and discussion questions.

However, I also realize the importance of exposing my congregation to a range of great teachers. Not only do I point them to particular pastors, authors, and speakers who have shaped me, I encourage them to learn with me.

The Let's Know the Bible Conference has become one such opportunity for my church. Attending with several other local congregations, we spend the day with our Bibles open, highlighters ready, and questions bubbling to the surface. This year we will get a ground floor picture of Isaiah from Dr. Bob Chisholm. My interest is already piqued. Perhaps I'll even bring my children.

© January 15, 2016

HOW PREACHING BUILDS CONFIDENCE IN THE BIBLE

by Aaron Hoak

Senior Pastor of Grace Baptist Church

Chances are you have a Bible within arm's reach. And if there's not a physical copy in sight, a swipe or a click will bring the Bible to the same screen you're using to read this post. We don't have to think about access to the Scriptures. With ease, and perhaps little appreciation for the privilege, we read the Bible, study it, and preach it.

In theory, we do this because we believe God has spoken to us from heaven through his Son (Hebrews 1:2; 12:25). That truth has been set down in writing, translated, and mass-produced. But does easy access to or familiarity with the Scriptures diminish our amazement or even confidence that we hold in our hands the very Word of God?

Part of the regular work of the pastor should help us at this point: diligent study of God's Word. Since I am privileged to bring a weekly sermon, I must study the Bible. It is my calling to stand and preach a message not of my own whims and opinions but of careful exposition and application of what God has said. Disciplined study teaches pastors to fade to the background and give center stage to God's Word.

Moreover, careful study increases the pastor's appreciation for *and* confidence in the Scriptures. As we dig into the Bible, we see the beauty of God's truth and character. We see sweet harmony in a canon of sixty-six inspired books spanning thousands of years, kingdoms, cultures, and languages. We see the personality of human authors bubbling through while the Divine author is never invisible. We see prophecy fulfilled. We see, from cover to cover, one main story—salvation—and one main character—Jesus, Son of

God. And we are drawn to worship this good and gracious God who has spoken through his Son.

Appreciation for and confidence in God's Word increase as we witness the fruits of effective preaching: sinners saved and lives transformed into the likeness of Christ. We see that the Word *is* living and active (Hebrews 4:12) and *does* accomplish God's purpose (Isaiah 55:11). That is a recipe for increased confidence in the Word of God.

Since we're fallen creatures in a fallen world, this isn't a linear process. We won't *always* see the beauty that's there; we won't *always* want to worship; people won't *always* be affected after we've diligently studied and preached. So we must be careful not to rest biblical confidence in feelings or the effects of preaching, but the revelation of God's Son. He is the final Word.

Instead of familiarity breeding contempt as we engage in careful study and preaching of God's truth, it should breed confidence. There is no book like the Bible. There is no revelation like God's Son. Preaching not only reflects this confidence, but also aims to implant it into the congregation, whose members may reap the fruit of greater faith, hope, and love.

© June 15, 2017

OUR MINISTER IN HEAVEN (HEBREWS 8:1–2)

by Herbert W. Bateman IV

President of the Cyber-Center for Biblical Studies

The point of what we are saying is this: We do have such a high priest, who sat down at the right hand of the throne of the Majesty in heaven, and who serves in the sanctuary, the true tabernacle set up by the Lord, not by man."
(NIV)

Before I share some thoughts about Hebrews 8:1–2, let me say something first about Hebrews chapter eight.

Chapter eight expands the presentation about Jesus as royal priest introduced in chapter 7. The expansion begins in chapter 8 but ends in chapter 10. In chapter 8, Jesus is in heaven where he ministers (vv. 1–6). An important aspect of his ministry concerns the mediation of a better covenant, which he contrasts with the Mosaic covenant. This contrast draws from Jeremiah 31:31–34 (LXX 38: 31–34). Jeremiah divulges God's displeasure with his people, discloses the coming of a new covenant, and draws attention to the termination of the Mosaic covenant (vv. 7–13).

So Hebrews 8:1–2 underscores Jesus' ministry in heaven. Verses 1–2, as presented above in italic, tell me three important things about Jesus ministry.

First, Jesus is our "high priest." Earlier in Hebrews we learn that Jesus is not like the high priest or any appointed Levitical priest of the past, he is God's appointed *royal* high priest (cf. 5:4–6; 7:21–22) and superior to them all (cf. 7:23–28).

Second, Jesus has authority. The phrase "who sat down at the right hand of the throne of the Majesty in heaven" speaks about Jesus authority. In the ancient Near Eastern culture, iconic images present kings sitting at the right hand of a pagan god. They symbolized a king's honored position with that god and the king's rule sanction by the god. In the Old Testament, Davidic kings were also depicted as sitting at God's right hand (figuratively speaking) to symbolize his honored position as God's chosen leader to rule over Israel (Pss .2, 72, 110). Although God was enthroned in heaven (Pss. 2:4, 9:7, 29:10; Isa 6:1), God extended his rule on earth through the Davidic king (Pss. 80:17, 89:21). So what does Jesus have? He has ruling authority sectioned by God. Where does Jesus rule? Unlike Davidic kings of the past, Jesus rules from heaven and in God's presence.

Third, our royal high priest serves in God's sanctuary. The phrase "who serves in the sanctuary, the true tabernacle set up by the Lord, not by man" underscores what Jesus does. He "ministers" (λειτουργός). Similar words are used to describe angels worshiping and *ministering* in heaven (Heb. 1:7, 14) and priests *serving* in an earthly tabernacle (Heb. 9:21; 10:11). Jesus ministers, however, in "the true tabernacle" that God himself "set up" and "not man" (οὐκ ἄνθρωπος; cf. Heb. 8:5). So unlike priests who ministered in an earthly tabernacle, Jesus ministers in a heavenly one in the presence of the living God. His ministry is a superior one (cf. Heb. 8:6).

What strikes me about Hebrews 8:1–2 is simply this: I have a royal high priest, who rules and ministers in God's presence on my behalf. He is someone I can approach with confidence, receive mercy, and find the grace I need to make it though another day (cf. Heb. 4:16).

© March 30, 2016

Exegetical Guides for Translating the New Testament

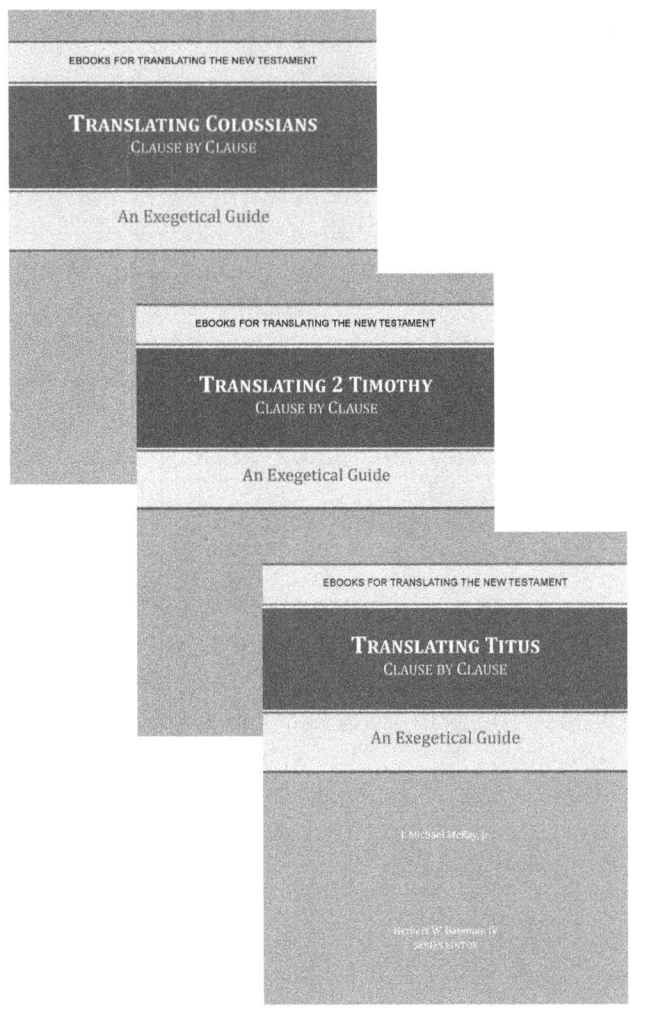

Designed as a translational guide, these CYBER-CENTER FOR BIBLICAL STUDIES eBooks for translating the New Testament isolate independent and dependent clauses, provide tips for translating New Testament letters, and share exegetical explanations to assist in the translation of biblical letters. Each book divides into three parts. First, an introduction prepares the reader for translating the letters. Second, letters are divided into manageable units of thought for translation purposes while providing contextual orientation for each unit. Finally, an answer key is provided with detailed exegetical explanations about each author's divisions and translations of the text.

Each book interacts with lexicons, grammars, and English translations in order to orient the translator to the challenges that come with translating New Testament letters. Yet the contextual orientation and clausal outlines enable the translator to trace the author's flow of thought in a manner that will be helpful for teaching and preaching purposes.

Ephesians by Benjamin I. Simpson

Philippians by Thomas S. Moore

Colossians by Adam Copenhaver

2 Timothy by Phillip A. Davis

Titus by J. Michael McKay Jr.

New **1 John** by Aaron C. Peer and Herbert W. Bateman IV

2 & 3 John by Aaron C. Peer and Herbert W. Bateman IV

Jude by Herbert W. Bateman IV

All volumes are available on Amazon

www.ingramcontent.com/pod-product-compliance
Lightning Source LLC
Chambersburg PA
CBHW081500040426
42446CB00016B/3329